A MAP THROUGH THE MAZE

A Guide to Surviving
the Criminal Justice System

by

Ned Rollo

with

Advice for Families of Offenders

by

Louis W. Adams, D.Min.

OPEN, INC. Information Series

SERIES EDITOR
Katherine S. Greene
OPEN, INC.

Dedicated to

Henry Langer

A Friend, Client, Benefactor, and Exceptionally Good Man

Who Paid His Dues, Took Control, and Put the System Behind Him

Rest In Peace

ABOUT THE AUTHORS

NED ROLLO

During the past 25 years, Ned Rollo has been active on both sides of the law. A "habitual criminal" and recovering addict, he takes the issue of success after prison very personally. After serving five and a half years in state and Federal prisons for manslaughter, narcotics, and firearms violations, he had to rebuild his life from scratch. Earning a degree from Roosevelt University, he has become a nationally known educator and correctional counselor helping other ex-offenders survive and prosper beyond the criminal justice experience.

Rollo founded OPEN, INC. in 1979 to teach survival skills to offenders and their families. To share his hard-won insight, he developed the OPEN Information Series—self-help handbooks which offer a sometimes painful but always honest view of what it takes to make it in the free world.

Part of the series, this book is based on the author's direct experience, along with the shared insight of over 25,000 offenders and loved ones he has helped. Rollo has paid the price to learn what works and the traps to avoid. His work, now in use across the country, offers a beacon of hope to millions of men and women who carry the label of "criminal."

LOUIS W. ADAMS

A minister and licensed professional counselor, Louis W. Adams certainly has the qualifications to help people in crisis. But his unique insight, concern, and sensitivity have made him especially effective as a counselor to offenders and families.

Dr. Adams earned his doctorate of ministry in pastoral counseling from Texas Christian University in 1975. At the same time, he gained hands-on experience and practical understanding of the needs of inmates and families while working as a chaplain with the Texas Dept. of Corrections from 1966 to 1974. He then practiced marriage and family therapy and finally served as director, clinical supervisor, and instructor for the Pastoral Care & Training Center at TCU from 1979 until his retirement in 1991.

Even after he left the prison system, prisoners' loved ones continued to seek Dr. Adams' guidance. His compassion and common sense have comforted countless family members and set them on the road to healthy coping.

FOREWORD

Since 1970, when as a young ex-convict he worked in a hostel for ex-prisoners in the Hyde Park district of Chicago where my family and I make our home, I have admired Ned Rollo and his dedication to helping those leaving prison make a useful life for themselves and for us.

In *A Map Through the Maze* he distills the knowledge and experience gained from his long and interesting journey of service. He knows whereof he writes, and he writes in a sprightly and compelling manner. He used his own bootstraps and a fine intelligence to pull himself up to a contributing life after five and a half years in prison; he now teaches others how to achieve five years of arrest-free behavior as the means of escape from the maze of convicthood. Self-image is the key; but self-image is to be shaped not by wishing it were so but by behaving so that it is so. The path Rollo has cleared for others to follow is shaped both by practical realities and by a sound psychological understanding.

It is a pleasure to be associated with this book. It stands in a noble tradition of respect for human endeavor, for recognition that there is a spark in all men and women that can be fanned to help shape a good life.

Norval Morris
Professor of Law and Criminology
University of Chicago

TABLE OF CONTENTS

OFFICIAL NOTICE

OPEN, INC. is a Texas nonprofit corporation founded in 1979 to improve public safety. This book is part of the *OPEN Information Series*, a developing collection of educational materials published under license from its copyright holder, V.N. Rollo, Jr.

All *Information Series* items are **privately produced**, representing only the viewpoint of the authors and OPEN, INC. Their content does not represent the official policy of any jail, prison, probation, or parole administration, or any other agency or individual.

INTRODUCTION

"Freedom is just another word for nothing left to lose."

A Map Through the Maze offers a rare, honest view into life in the criminal justice system. What is recorded here isn't so much about what one lives as it is about what one learns. Not the obvious stuff that anyone can see on a one-hour fish bowl tour through a prison, but the mental and emotional effects of waking up a thousand mornings in a cold concrete box. It is a grim reflection of real life and the quicksand one must wade through to survive. Like squatting naked in the corner of a solitary cell, it is what it is. You don't have to like it; you just have to deal with it!

If you're expecting the views of outside observers or well-intended squares, this book is not for you. Nor is it a collection of old war stories or wishful projections of how things are supposed to be. Instead, the focus of this book is freedom: the most basic concern of every prisoner in the world. We look at what freedom means, how to build it, and how to keep it. The contents are based on the direct experiences and insights of thousands of outlaws and social rejects: some who died in a cage and others who are living well in the free world.

You will find that freedom is a complex issue. There are no simple answers. The liberty to think and do as we wish is one of the great treasures of life. Yet we appreciate it most when we have it least. Too often it is more of an illusion than a fact. In reality freedom is never total, and it is surely never free. But for the legions of men and women "under supervision" this hour, freedom is the main goal of daily life. Not just physical liberty, but freedom of mind and spirit as well.

Once defined as a criminal and locked away, you are at the bottom of a thousand-foot well. From there, the world is but a tiny dot of light. It takes great effort and supreme commitment to climb to the surface and once again know the joy of a spring breeze. First you must learn to master the heavy, insane changes that come with the process of American justice. From arrest, through court and captivity, to long after release, the journey often seems an endless maze of huge barriers and deadly traps. People labeled as criminals and their families wage a constant battle to survive. Theirs is an uphill path of fear, fragile hope, and daily distress. To succeed takes unique insight, courage, and skill.

Along with the plight of offenders, we have a special concern for families and loved ones who try so hard and give up so much. Those who struggle to stand by persons caught in the corrections process are often totally alone and taken for granted. They are called upon to perform legal miracles, drive 12 hours to spend an hour with a hostile inmate, and on top of everything else, not complain. So, for those who love a prisoner and are called upon to jump tall buildings, pay the bills, and write every day, this book is for you, too. Keep it close by to review when you get lost. It will improve your welfare and peace of mind.

Family members and loved ones who study this book will get a good feel for the changes an offender goes through. This offers a way to "look inside the head" of prisoners as they move from one stage and mood to another. It helps take away a lot of the stress of always wondering what's going on and why. At the same time it offers inmates valuable insight into the intense changes faced by those loved ones as they wait and worry.

A Map Through the Maze is a very special guidebook, offering training and support to help solve problems, cope with hardship, and maintain hope. You will learn the mental and social stages people go through and the outlook needed to survive. But beyond mere survival, this is a guide to obtaining true freedom through personal growth. It points out ways to finish the trip stronger, wiser, and better able to control your future. At the end of the journey, you can have a better grasp of the nature of freedom and ways to let it expand in your life.

To make sense out of the maze, this book is broken into four parts. First, an inmate's look at the nature of freedom. Next, how to "beat the system" through personal growth. Third, a hard-core tour through the correctional experience. And, last, some very special advice on how families and loved ones can overcome grief, hold on, and get healthy.

THE NATURE OF FREEDOM

"Man, freedom is being able to saddle up and ride off into the sunset!"

JUST CUT ME LOOSE!

Ask any prisoner what he or she wants more than anything else and the answer is automatic: "**OUT!**" Nose first or toes first, everyone wants to be free!

Most people would say that freedom means being able to do what you want, when you want to. Yet if you stop and look at it, this is romantic nonsense. Reality **never** permits us to be totally free. What we do always has limits, both in the joint and in the "free world." Laws of nature restrict what we can do physically, in addition to the social boundaries created by the people and society around us. Not everyone can be president, walk on the moon, make a million dollars, or gain the love of the person they desire.

Freedom will *always* be limited because we can't control the forces of nature, the rules of society, or the choices of other people. However, between the extremes of total liberty and total slavery is a vast area in which a person can govern his or her own fate. This is especially true of the ways we treat ourselves and others and in the values we elect to live by. While we always seek maximum freedom, the quality of our lives will be determined by how well we strike a *balance* between our desires and the limits of reality.

Free But Not Free

What if a person had all the money, power, and possessions they could desire, and society would let them do as they pleased: would they then be truly free? No, it would still be an illusion because our freedom is limited from birth by the certainty that we will die. NO ONE is free from aging, suffering, and death.

And even if we could be free of all these external chains, we can still be enslaved by *ourselves*. Our thoughts and feelings, desires and fears can entrap us just as surely as steel bars. Our level of freedom depends not just on the condition of our body and the world we live in, but also on the state of our mind and what we carry *within* us: what we think and how we feel about ourselves and everything around us. If we don't learn to control how we think and feel, then we are mere **robots**, directed by whatever ideas and emotions run through us.

For instance, no matter where you are, if you are eaten up with anger or greed, you are not free. Why? Because you are being controlled by the force of that rage and lust within yourself. Your choices and actions are based on those powerful emotions—not on what is best for you or most truly fulfills your goals and intentions. You may really desire a close, loving relationship, but if anger runs your life, you will wall yourself off from others and drive them away. As long as anger controls you, you are not free to be the person you want to be.

For another example, if you build your life on falsehood—on what you imagine things to be rather than what they really are—you become a slave to *illusion*. You may be free to make choices, but your freedom to act is still limited because you don't really understand yourself or the world around you. As long as your view of yourself and the world is distorted, you will be a captive of your own ignorance.

All prisoners long for freedom, but often we don't face the traps hiding within ourselves. We just sit and dream of the day of release. And in the process we collect centuries worth of hostility, false goals, fear, distrust, and self-hatred. In reality, we build our *own* personal prison and sentence ourselves to death by lethal aloneness. There has to be a better way!

TRUE FREEDOM

"True freedom comes when you see past illusion and respond to life and yourself as they really are."

Just as we can be slaves to the world or to ourselves, we also can achieve immense freedom. Although external liberty depends on what the world around us will let us do, our internal freedom is based on the health and power of our own minds and wills. In fact, the only thing we can truly control is ourselves! Therefore, the only place we can really be free is inside our own minds and hearts. We can have true freedom when we come to terms with ourselves and dedicate our efforts to personal growth and positive action.

To be truly free, we must learn to rule our thoughts and feelings, not be ruled by them. We must refuse to be trapped in hate, fear, lust, or knee-jerk reactions to outside events. We must not fool ourselves with distorted ideas. Instead we must look at ourselves and the world clearly and honestly, so that our thoughts and actions are based on reality, not illusion. We must pull our own strings, and not let anyone or anything do it for us.

It's only when you don't know what you stand for that someone else can come into your head and shove you around. When you have a clear picture of what's real and what you believe in, people play hell pushing your buttons! Once you have your own internal rules clearly defined, you can learn to adapt to the rules of both the joint and the streets without losing your identity or self-worth. Remember: although you can't control what happens—in the maze or in the streets— you *can* learn to control how you think about and react to it. *This* is the secret to freedom in an unfree world!

Since prisoners are social outcasts, you must remember that your true power and worth exist within yourself. Your quality is not based on what other people think or do. Instead it depends on the nature of your inner self and the values you carry within, no matter if your body is in a lockdown cell in Leavenworth or on a sun-drenched beach on the French Riviera. When someone commands your body, they have the least of you; but if they control your mind or break your spirit, they have ALL of you! For this reason, you must be ever vigilant. Always respect your mind and heart and be ready to protect them from confusion and illusion, whether created by you or by outside forces.

A clear mind with truth as its goal is one of the most important qualities we can develop in the quest for a rewarding life. Without it, all the physical freedom and fortune in the world mean **nothing**. While our bodies exist on only a few levels, the scope of our minds and spirits is *boundless*. We are capable of an infinite variety of possible paths.

With the right direction and force of will, we can cast aside the chains of ignorance and suffering and learn to soar. "Come on, even in a stinking cage?" Yes, even in the darkest, foulest dungeon on this planet!

MAKING YOURSELF FREE

Mankind has learned to make atomic bombs and walk in space, but the ability to direct our thoughts and values is the greatest power we have as humans. Outside forces can hold, chain, or even torture our bodies but they cannot control our minds unless we surrender them! This most powerful and useful form of freedom is beyond the grasp of anyone outside us. The **ONLY** way to get it is by dedication and work. No one else can give it to us, and likewise no one can take it away unless we permit it.

You don't have to be a genius or have a masters degree to be mentally free. But you must learn to tell the difference between fact and falsehood, between what is real and what is not. In a world that is 99% jive, finding the 1% that is real is the basis for freeing yourself. Then you need the honesty, courage, and will power to apply your insight in positive, productive ways.

To do this, in prison or on the streets, we must constantly practice self-discovery and self-mastery. To free our minds, we have to seek out real truth; this requires that we openly test what we believe, discard what we find to be false, and then adopt what is more factual and useful. The greatest thief of our freedom is our own narrow vision and unbending ignorance.

For example, many of us were raised with strong biases against people of different races or beliefs. This keeps us apart from others, creating unnecessary fear, suspicion, and even hate. Yet as adults we often find someone of a different color or religion who is honest, decent, and good. We may find, to our shock, that we actually like and respect this person, although we were raised to mistrust and dislike him or her.

How do we come to terms with this conflict of our past ideas and the present reality? We must examine ourselves, question the things we were raised to blindly believe, then seek to discover how things *really are* and how they *should be*. Our capacity to sort out for ourselves true from false and right from wrong is unique to the human mind. And this ability offers a type of freedom FAR more powerful than anything on a physical plane.

As you move through the stages of the system, you will come across parts of yourself enslaved by ideas contrary to fact. You will not want to change and may strongly resist coming to terms with truth and justice; this is just part of being human. But it is *essential* that you have the courage and flexibility to grow.

A CHOICE TO GROW

"The choice is simple: grow or die."

Being a "guest of the system" can drive you crazy, but it can also "drive you sane" in special ways. There is nothing like a jailhouse to help you examine your views and values. While free world folks are busy with concerns like tread on their tires and braces on a kid's teeth, prisoners and their loved ones often deal with sheer get-down survival. Living in the maze calls time out on trivial everyday issues and brings you face to face with the here and now. One thing for sure: it offers a chance to stop and think—to reflect on the nature of life and your place in it.

Hard times in general will force you to look into the deeper parts of yourself. But it is an even greater challenge when your vision is distorted by the madness of the criminal justice maze. It takes super-human dedication and effort to grow tall enough mentally to see over the mountains of mental garbage, brick walls, and rows of razor wire which confine you. Whenever you find something which keeps you lost in the darkness and confusion, dedicate yourself to finding a better path, no matter how much effort it requires.

Part of the wonderful power of our minds is the ability to change what we think, what we value, and how we react. When we find something that just isn't true or doesn't work, we have what it takes to alter our beliefs and responses. As we grow mentally, we can eventually develop the wisdom to see and respond to things *as they truly are*. This is what it takes to find your way out of the maze and never come back.

Growth in a cage requires limitless courage and sweat, but great progress is possible. Throughout history, times of imprisonment and hardship have driven people to discover and focus their inner spirit. I am referring to something much deeper, more honest and real than simply trying to pray your way out of a joint. Spiritual awareness is the extension of our minds beyond time and space into the highest levels of being to which we as humans are capable.

This is one of the positive aspects of fighting through the maze: when it expands our understanding of our higher nature. It's too long, hard, and dangerous for anyone to survive and exit without immense courage, honesty, and discipline. So, unless you are content to live and die as human road kill, you have no choice but to pay the price and unlock the freedom of your mind and spirit!

In the next section **Beating the System**, we will look at what it takes to outgrow the system. Above all else, you must remember that *it can be done* and *you can do it!*

BEATING THE SYSTEM

"Little brother, beating the system is the name of this game!"

Every convict searches for ways to defeat the "system." But just how does a person **really** get over? I've asked myself this question for 26 years. Do you become a jail house lawyer or a militant reformer, dig a hole under the east wall, or do dope deals over the pay phones? Or are there better ways? Just what does one have to do to "beat the system"?

If you go to war with the Man, what happens? In comes the goon squad to strum on your head. If it's a riot, up drives the national guard. If the weekend warriors cannot do the trick, they call in the army to drop the hammer. The body count is always the same. The Man: a few, mostly innocent bystanders. Convicts: *MANY*, most also just innocent bystanders. Therefore, direct physical assault achieves *nothing* but a blood bath. Plus it gives the administration an excuse to tighten the screws yet another turn!

Note: I am not saying you should just roll over and play dead. But be careful not to draw your sword and step off into quicksand. Maintaining your dignity is one thing, but setting yourself up for a fresh dime or a load of 00 buckshot is just plain silly. If you really think that making your problems worse is a way to make them better, I suggest you reconsider. I know one con whose way of getting over was to make a hundred grand selling truck loads of dope from inside the walls. He actually did it. Of course, he is still doing the extra 25 years without parole they dropped on him. In the end the only thing he "beat" was himself.

So if you really want to beat the system, two things are necessary: **you've got to out-live them and outgrow them!** This means using every drop of energy and every opportunity to improve yourself on *every possible level*. Because until you learn to grow beyond the maze, you are doomed to remain a resident of some high security tomb with well-polished floors.

GROWTH IS THE KEY

"Change is certain, growth is optional."

Change Is Certain

Going to prison is like being sent to a hostile alien planet, where you face a long series of extreme hardships and strange, unnatural ways of thinking and acting. It's a three-shift graveyard full of distant memories and false dreams. A prisoner looks around and thinks, "There ain't **nothing** happening here but fools talking trash!" And, in fact, all you actually see and hear are people constantly shuffling to cope with day-to-day survival.

But that's only on the surface of things. While every day brings the same old boring routine, what's going on *inside* of people never stands still. Like any war zone, a prison is a place which **demands** change! The question is, what types of changes are going to occur inside of YOU? Will they be positive or negative? Useful or harmful? Will you come out of it better able to cope and be content, or end up a stone basket case?

Growth Is Optional

Simply existing and watching yourself get old doesn't take any special ability. It happens all by itself. The real challenge is having the will and skill to make use of change to advance yourself and make your life more rewarding. This advancement or positive change is what we are going to call "growth." It is the most powerful tool a convict has, both during and following prison.

Lying around in prison feeling like a zombie, you may tell yourself that growth is impossible, that the best you can hope to do is make it from hour to hour. This is a normal result of depression and self-pity, but in reality nothing could be farther from the truth. Fact: if we are not *actively working* to control and use the constant changes we experience, then we have surrendered our lives and become mere zoo animals. Growth is so much more than just existing! Simply existing—just letting your fingernails grow while the rest of you stays in a coma—is like being dead but too lazy to fall over.

Listen to me: the way to *really* beat the Man is to **GROW!** Growth of the total person: mind, body, and spirit. This means learning to control and direct yourself in order to rise above the madness and sadness of the moment. For a "guest of the government," *personal development is the one and only path to success!*

There is not some switch you can flip and suddenly you're on top of the growth game. Rather, **growth is a process of becoming**. This means active, determined pursuit of knowledge and a better way of doing things. To grow, you must seek out new, exciting ways to make your life and yourself ever more useful, content, and glad to be alive. Your rewards are *progress* and *pride*. In this way you can learn to celebrate life NOW, even from inside a steel cage.

You Must Decide

> *"No matter what I have to face, I owe it to myself to develop my abilities to the greatest degree possible."*

Grow or stagnate: the choice is yours. No other single decision has as great an impact on the outcome of life. In fact, it is this very choice that allows you to seek true freedom, in prison and in the free world.

As a prisoner, you have little control over what you do and how you do it. Your options are very limited. But you **do** have total control over your decision to advance yourself or just to sit around and decay. This advancement can be academic, vocational, artistic, spiritual, cultural, emotional, or in many other areas. Much can be achieved by simply taking an honest look into yourself! The point is that you deliberately **choose** to apply your mind and energy to positive, creative issues.

Everyone faces this choice. But why do some people fight to grow, even under the worst of conditions, while others simply give up? In truth this is one of the great riddles of life. But the answer to this mystery is the key required to unlock your shackles. Therefore it is worth whatever price you must pay to discover an answer within yourself.

The Source of Power

"The power of a mind totally committed exceeds any other force on earth."

What it takes to beat the system is an inner drive to focus on personal growth. Without this focus, the negative forces in and around us will decide who and what we are. And the world will look on and say, "Poor Joe. He never had a chance." No—poor Joe never *made* a chance for himself.

The quest for freedom demands a **total commitment** to doing our best with the cards we have been dealt. There must be an inner drive to grow, to become the best that we can be. No one knows why this drive is stronger in some people than in others, but it is the central reason that we see some people as successes in life while others fail.

People have lots of excuses for not growing. Many folks have a poor education, bad upbringing, lack of family support, physical or mental disabilities. But most problems can be overcome, partly if not entirely. There are blind lawyers, one-legged skiers, paraplegic horseback riders, mentally retarded college students, and successful ex-cons. Overcoming obstacles takes tremendous determination and hard work, but it can be done.

In reality, there is *no* excuse for not growing. In the long run, it isn't any easier to sit around waiting to die than it is to get up and make something of your life. Yes, growth takes discipline, courage, and hard work. But not growing means that you have to face the same problems over and over again. Problems never go away until you learn to solve them. In general, they just keep on getting worse. If you're going to be facing problems anyway, you might as well put your energy into solving them rather than wasting your time trying to escape them.

You owe it to yourself to make your life the best it can be. No doubt it's hard work to get an education; but it's even harder to make a living without one. It's not easy keeping fit and healthy; but it's sure better than being too sick and weak to take care of business. And if you put your energy into growing rather than trying to hide from life, you will be rewarded by a tremendous sense of pride and achievement. This is a reward you can look forward to when you get tired and start wondering why you are pushing yourself so hard.

NO ESCAPE FROM OURSELVES!

In order to grow, we have to start where we are. Although we may not be satisfied with our current condition, the person we are now is the raw material for our transformation. If the results of our behavior are unrewarding for us and the people around us, then it's time to find a better way to interact with the world.

One area in our lives that probably needs a lot of work is problem-solving. The demands of life, both in prison and on the streets, are often extreme, complex, and seemingly overpowering. A state of crisis doesn't allow for a lot of time and patience; conditions seem to demand an instant response. When the pressure gets great enough, we often blow up and do the first thing that occurs to us in order to get immediate relief.

This knee-jerk reaction gets rid of the intense stress we were feeling, and it may fix or postpone the problem for a while. But many situations, feelings, and problems have no instant solution. We are just creating new negative results to be faced in the future. The original problem is not solved, only delayed; it will come back to haunt us even worse than before. And we forfeit the growth, pride, and peace of mind that come when we solve a problem and move on.

Reacting to the here and now without regard for the long-term effects of our actions **just doesn't work!** But often we keep on repeating the same behavior over and over again. We have a strong tendency to believe that if something doesn't work, then we need to do more of it. It is amazing the effort we will make to continue old ways of thinking and acting which hurt us, rather than face the fear and discomfort of the unknown. And the deeper and older the issues, the more we hold on to how things have always been.

To make things even worse, we feel like a failure. This feeling of being a "loser" may be the worst result of all. It follows us like a black cloud, constantly affecting the way we see ourselves. In this deadly state of mind, we lose hope of making any real progress and frankly see ourselves as lower than gorilla snot. We have trapped ourselves in a cycle of self-destructive behavior.

Such counter-productive action is especially obvious if we are addicted to some substance, thought process, emotional rush, or type of behavior. We use the addictive behavior to relieve our stress, but it won't make our problems go away. They just get worse, plus we have to cope with new problems—physical, financial, legal, and in our relationships—created by the addiction.

If this is the story of your life, it's time for a change. Change is hard and it can be very frightening. *But there's no escape.* You can keep on struggling with the same old problems which keep getting worse, or you can put all that wasted energy into your efforts to control and improve your fate. You owe it to yourself—and to the people who care about you—to choose the path toward growth and freedom.

Barriers to Growth

Making a commitment to grow and improve your life allows you to work toward a better future, but it won't be easy. All humans have a natural resistance to change. No matter how deadly they are, your old ways of doing things are familiar; they seem to offer comfort and security. Doing away with them can be deeply disturbing. In order to carry out your commitment to yourself, you will have to face and overcome many of the following barriers to growth.

a. **Fear** is a powerful enemy of positive change. It can come in many forms, such as fear of failure, fear of rejection, fear of the unknown, even fear of change itself. In a way, when we think about changing a basic belief or pattern of behavior, it seems as if we will have to give up our true selves. We may fear change almost the way we would fear dying. We may not believe that we can be the same person if we change the way we think and act.

   Solution: One way to confront fear is to ask yourself what is the worst that could happen if your fear comes true. Many times, this is no worse than what you have now. Then decide what is the best possible outcome if you face your fear. Now that you already know the worst that can happen, concentrate on the positive outcomes you can achieve by overcoming your fears. Realize that the person you are working to become is truly you; you are just freeing up more of your potential self. Keep these thoughts in mind so that you can control your fear rather than it controlling you.

b. **Denial** is a defense mechanism we use to block out any ideas we aren't prepared to deal with. It is a mental trick that keeps us from facing reality and making the changes we need to become better people. If we don't admit to ourselves that we have a problem or limitation, we can just glide along until something forces us to deal with it. If there is really a "devil," it is denial, because it keeps us content with our own ignorance!

   Solution: Be painfully honest with yourself. And if someone suggests you have a problem, take heed; don't just blow it off or make excuses. Other people can sometimes see what is going on in your life more clearly than you can. Don't be discouraged by admitting you have problems or issues that need work; this is the first step to solving them. In the end, it takes ten times more energy trying to ignore the true nature of things than it does to face reality and take positive action.

c. **Impatience** is an age-old barrier to growth. By wanting too much too soon, we set ourselves up to fail. This is a major trap and the source of much anxiety, both short- and long-term, for ex-convicts and their loved ones.

   Solution: Break your goal down into small achievable tasks. Then you can pat yourself on the back as you achieve each step. Remind yourself that it takes *time* to make positive changes. The process can't be rushed along based on your wishes. Time will never bend itself to your needs, so you have to plan ahead and use it to your advantage. Take many small steps, not just a few big ones. In this way, change will become your friend and ally.

d. **Unrealistic** goals set us up to fail by focusing our energy on things that we can't achieve or things that will harm us, not help us. Trying to do the impossible keeps us from achieving the possible, wasting energy we need for growth.

    Solution: Always remember that wanting what you cannot or should not have is the Number One enemy of all prisoners and loved ones. Test your goals with intense honesty and seek advice from people with wisdom, maturity, and direct experience. Above all else: really think things through before you make a decision.

e. **Dependencies** or addictions drain us of the power and mental focus we need to change and grow. We must free ourselves from our anchors in order to best face the future.

    Solution: First, overcome your denial and admit the effect your addiction is having on you. Then seek help to gain control over the forces which command you. Such problems seldom go away by themselves; they demand attention, work, support, and a great deal of courage and resolve. You can do it— and you'll be real glad you did!

f. **Fatal Attachments** to other people create a special form of addiction that keeps us distracted and drained of energy and focus. A relationship out of balance can be far worse than any drug habit. It can lead to untold misery and despair.

    Solution: Learn what it takes to build a healthy, positive relationship (see **Personal Ties** on page 28). Study rewarding ways to deal with others and build true friendships. Then look honestly at how you relate to people. If your relationships aren't positive, resolve to improve them. If you can't— *then let them go*. Remember, good friends support positive growth. They don't double-dare you to sabotage yourself.

g. **Anger, Guilt, Isolation, and Worry** are negative feelings which soak up our energy and focus it in a negative direction. Each is a form of "baggage" we've collected to defend ourselves from dealing with our hurts and fears. Although they seem unpleasant, these feelings can become addictions that we use to avoid facing reality. Then we end up wasting our power on useless battles rather than working to grow and prosper.

    Solution: Let go of past resentments and focus on future growth. Work to replace anger with peace of mind, guilt with forgiveness, and isolation with a sense of oneness with all beings. This won't happen overnight. It is a gradual by-product of your success in improving the way you deal with yourself and the world. It is well worth the effort!

h. **Hopelessness** is the greatest enemy to growth. Without hope, we tend to just give up. I saved this till last because it often occurs as a result of the problems stated above. We can afford to lose many things and still be able to function, but the loss of hope is the last straw.

Solution: Reach down into the center of your mind, the core of your spirit, to find your connection with the power and wonder of the universe. Call upon your primitive instincts for the strength of will to survive. And never surrender your faith in beauty and your commitment to making the very best of your life. *Never give up!!*

You will certainly run into some or all of these barriers as you focus on your personal development. At times the barriers to change may seem overwhelming, but you must *never* give up. One of your rewards will be the satisfaction of knowing how hard you had to work for your progress. You deserve the best life you can make for yourself. And now is your chance get started on a better path. Like a cell partner once said, "The day you quit beating your head against the wall, you begin to feel better **immediately**!"

INSIDE THE RAZOR WIRE

"Humpty Dumpty sat on the wall, Humpty Dumpy took a GREAT fall. All the King's horses and all the King's men couldn't put Humpty together again. But Humpty could, and he did! What a guy!!"

In order to overcome obstacles and make positive changes, you must first know how. So what are the basic attitudes you must adopt before you can come to grips with yourself?

Accept Yourself

No one is born with an Instruction Manual on being human. Who you are is the result of your past: what you have observed and what you have been taught, as well as the choices you've made. Many of your attitudes and values were formed when you were very young, so you may have no real idea WHY you think and behave the way you do.

Sometimes your actions are positive, constructive, and rewarding—other times they are not. If you honestly examine your life, you may have to admit that some of your behavior caused great harm for others as well as yourself. It can be very painful to admit this, but you can't change what happened in the past. Getting lost in a guilt trip or fantasies about what could have been is just a waste of time. It ties up all the energy you could put into making the future better.

In order to grow, you must first recognize and accept who you are **now**. Trying to hide from yourself is simply a roadblock on the path of progress. Rather than dwelling on what you have done wrong, it helps to view your past actions as mistakes you made because you hadn't learned enough. At the same time, you must be absolutely determined to learn and grow from the results and do better next time. To screw up is a natural part of life, but to look for new ways to repeat the same errors is crazy.

Accept Responsibility

Just as it is wasteful to wallow in guilt, it is equally useless to make excuses or blame your actions on someone or something else. There may be many reasons for what you have done, but in the final count, you are where you are because of the choices you made. And believe it or not, this is good. After all, if everything you do is somebody else's fault, then you will never be free and in control of your life.

Tattoo this across your brain: if you don't want someone else running your show, you have to do it for yourself. When you waste energy trying to avoid responsibility for yourself, you just become weaker and more vulnerable to control by the State and many other people and things. Many folks surrender and just go with the flow, simply existing as a robot for the forces around them. Running your own show is serious business; you must take control of yourself if you want to protect and develop your freedom and dignity.

Since **you** are responsible for what you do, it's a good time to develop or expand the skills and insights you need to handle yourself. Learn to better understand your feelings, control your responses, and plan your actions. As you get yourself more in hand, you will find less grief and more satisfaction in life.

Understand Cause and Effect

The first rule of reality which governs *everything* is the law of cause and effect. We have all heard the expressions "you reap what you sow" and "what goes around comes around." Nothing could be more true! In fact, the quality of our lives ultimately depends on how well we apply the law of cause and effect.

This is not some game we can play just when we feel like it. It is an inescapable fact of nature. If someone touches a hot stove, he or she gets burned: that is direct and simple to understand. But cause and effect is always functioning, even when we don't see the effects directly or immediately. For example, people who are exposed to the AIDS virus (cause) may seem healthy for years before they develop cancers and other serious illnesses (effect).

The law of cause and effect is in operation with *each* thought and action. When we learn what kinds of effects follow which causes, we can plan our actions in order to improve our fate and grow beyond our past mistakes. When we finally realize that everything we do comes back to us, suddenly it makes good sense to think good thoughts and do good deeds.

By coming to grips with the no-jive reality of cause and effect, we find the key to unlock a positive, rewarding future. It is a powerful and life-changing moment when we finally accept the fact that our actions ultimately control *our* fate. This is a two-edged sword: it makes us responsible for our failures as well as our successes. It also offers *true hope* for personal growth and fulfillment.

Seek the Right Path

So far we have been discussing *how* to accept responsibility for ourselves and change our lives for the better. But the central issue is, what are we going to become? What is the goal of our growth? This is a question of our ***values***, what we believe to be right, true, and important.

Developing your values is a very personal, internal choice. No one can get inside of you to change them. You have to do it yourself. Society may tell you what values you ought the choose, and even punish you for making a different choice, but the final decision will be up to you.

In India three thousand years ago, seekers of the right path had this to say about values:

> *"We are what our deep, driving desire is. As our deep, driving desire is, so is our will. As our will is, so is our deed. As our deed is, so is our destiny." (Brihadaranyaka IV.4-5)*

So our values determine who we are and who we will become. But since everyone views life differently, how do we figure out what is really right, true, and important? As we examine our past values and behavior and make choices on which direction our growth will take, we must always remember that some ways of thinking and acting work better than others. By looking at human history we can see that some ways usually have "good" (constructive, helpful) results, while others almost always have "bad" (destructive, harmful) results.

Of all the advice for establishing good values, perhaps none is more practical or down-to-earth than the Golden Rule: treat other people as you want to be treated. Living by the Golden Rule doesn't guarantee that you will always be treated well. But it does add to the good will available in the world and makes it possible for more positive things to happen for everyone.

Many people in our society would say that love of God, country, and family are the most important values. Many would say that we should be generous, help others, and obey the law. That it is more important to be honest, fair, and helpful to others than it is to get what we want out of life. These values are considered good because they usually have helpful, constructive results.

However, if we look at what people do, we may see different values in action. We often see people for whom money and material possessions—or power, respect, and attention from others—are the most important values. Some people skirt society's rules or maybe bend them without breaking the law. Other people don't care if they hurt others or break the law to get what they want.

These values are more likely to be considered bad because their results are generally less helpful or even destructive. However, it seems as if these values would get us what we want faster and easier than being good. So if we choose good values, what's in it for us?

First: a path out of the criminal justice maze. You stand a much better chance of staying out of prison through helpful actions than through harmful behavior. Also, you can expect much more peace of mind if you're not always looking over your shoulder for the law to grab you or figuring an angle to put something over on an unsuspecting square. You will find a greater degree of social acceptance for positive behavior than for negative actions. And you will end up with greater self-respect: positive thoughts and actions give us good feelings about ourselves, and this is what makes everything else worthwhile.

Understand, I'm not suggesting that you do good for everyone else at the expense of yourself. Instead, make constructive choices that bring about the most positive results for you *and* for those around you. Look for ways to create an all-win situation. Choose actions that allow you to fulfill your potential and produce something useful for yourself and others. Practice behavior that helps you form close, rewarding relationships with other people. Pursue thoughts and actions that make you feel truly valuable and at peace with yourself.

Eventually, you may find that your greatest personal satisfaction comes from knowing you have met your obligations—to other people as well as yourself—and that you have left the world a better place. This kind of gift to mankind will last far beyond your own life, while any power and possessions you collect will just pass to someone else when you're gone.

MAKING THE SYSTEM WORK FOR YOU

If you want to grow beyond the system, it's time to get started right now. There's no point in waiting till later. The day you hit the streets is way too late!

Look at it this way: prison isn't an experience to be wasted. Every moment is so dumb and destructive that it *must* be put to practical use so you can salvage some value from it. Rather than just sitting around playing dominos or watching TV, why not focus on personal development? Improve your ability to meet your needs, assist others, and feel better about yourself. Can you think of any more meaningful way to beat the system?

Learning Through Hardship

As we've said, taking a fall helps a person stop and look at the direction and meaning of life. While citizens are concerned with Monday night football, you have a chance to examine the deepest parts of your mind and heart. What you find, you may not like. If that's the case, you have the time to pull yourself together and *change it!*

Jails and prisons are places of intense pressure and, like all war zones, produce intense change. For better or worse, no one gets to stand still. What kind of shape are you going to be in when they finally kick you out? It may well depend on what direction you're taking this very moment.

Surviving and growing beyond the prison experience is not an easy task. In fact, it's more like an obstacle course—it's painful to go through, but it helps us develop greater strength and new skills. It takes time and effort to make it over the hurdles, but we sure have a clear knowledge of our abilities by the end of the course. We only lose if we give up or try to go around the obstacles; we've spent all that time and effort, and still learned nothing for our trouble. So let's look at the state of mind and spirit needed to survive and grow from it all.

Reshape Your Thinking

As a prisoner, you may often feel like you're trapped in a zoo. Be aware that there are mental tools and ways of looking at things that can be your salvation. First, always remember that this occurrence had a beginning and will have an end. Even if it's in a pine box, you *will* get out. For most people, being labeled a criminal is only one chapter in life. It's really up to you if you want to take the brand of "outcast" to your grave. Surely it's not necessary! The secret is to learn new ways of thinking and develop control over your thoughts and actions. This is an achievement of untold worth! Think about it....

1) You are human, not some wild animal driven by blind instinct. STOP AND THINK BEFORE YOU ACT! Being controlled by the State is demanding, but learning to control *yourself* is a thousand times harder. There is no greater challenge anyone can face than coming to grips with their thoughts, emotions, and behaviors. Learn to **watch** the way your mind works, **study** the effects, **control** your emotions, and you will grow to better **direct** your actions. Your growing insight will allow you to make positive changes in your life.

2) Realize that you are not limited to one fixed way of doing things: *you have choices.* Telling yourself that you cannot cope or have no way out leads to mental illness and spiritual decay. Be creative; make a list of *all* the possible ways to solve your problem. Reach out for positive ideas and new ways to cope. When you learn to look and listen, you'll find that the options you need come from the most unexpected people and at the most unexpected times. Stay alert, flexible, and receptive.

3) Review your options and consider the possible outcomes for each. Which one has the best chance of granting positive, winning results? And I don't mean just immediate, short-term relief; not a mere "fix" but a real solution. Beware: anything that makes your problems worse is self-destructive!

4) Apply your decision and give it plenty of time to work. Don't expect instant relief because that's just not real. It took serious time and thought to make your decision, so give it a serious chance to work. When it comes to solving problems, you must have plenty of faith and patience.

5) Usually we have to deal with things in stages, like the seasons of the year. When working on a complex problem, you can divide it into manageable parts and better control the results. This is equally true for getting a job, overcoming an addiction, or making a good marriage. Spending time and energy to work through a problem helps you be and feel better prepared. No matter how big the task or ambitious your plans, it always comes down to one step at a time!

6) Observe the results of what you think and do. Use the outcome to test your beliefs and modify your future actions. The only real "failure" is refusing to learn from your experiences. If you find that you keep making the same mistakes over and over, admit that you could use some help. It's OK to get help because staying stuck in a rut of failure and frustration is unnecessary and just plain stupid.

7) Give yourself credit for the progress you make. Celebrate your victories; take pride and satisfaction in every bit of achievement! And if you don't score a total success or things don't move as quickly as you'd like, for heaven's sake don't give up. Just keep on cooking!

Use What's There!

> *"Pounce on ANY source of positive energy like a duck on a June bug!"*

To improve your chances of success, use this time to develop an attitude and a plan which will increase your sense of personal control and satisfaction. Any chance you have to grow by expanding your mind or skills, any counseling you can get, any steps you can take to improve yourself—**DO IT!** Prisons are not known for their abundance of culture and opportunity, but you can usually find access to educational courses or vocational training, libraries, self-help groups, or visits from outside *volunteers*.

If you don't know how to read very well, *learn.* Absorb everything you can get your hands on that promotes your ability to do good business. Don't kick back on your rack and get lost in romance novels, westerns, or science fiction; they are great for practice and for killing time, but they don't push you to grow. Read and study things that *put time and your mind to work.* What you're looking for are new, fresh ideas that make you think, not just movie magazines and *Sports Illustrated* that put you to sleep.

Once you have made a total and unbending commitment to self-improvement and ultimate success, you can't afford to waste your valuable time and energy on the garbage going on around you. This sense of purpose, linked with discipline, is priceless as you wade through the distractions and folly of life in prison or in the free world. And believe it or not, learning this one skill can make the disaster of imprisonment a valuable experience.

Ya Snapped Yet?

> *"The freedom we seek begins with the decision to accept responsibility for the gift of life we have been granted."*

A lot of what happens during and after prison depends on a person's *attitude.* Having a "bad attitude" usually means being negative, hostile, or just an overall pain in the butt in a hundred different ways. Such people are NO FUN to be around and usually selfish to the bone.

But even worse, people with a bad attitude deceive and weaken themselves by blaming everything and everyone else for their problems. As prisoners watch one another, they see how people cope with what comes down. They learn to identify those who deal with reality and those who don't. Some inmates deal with things head on, find solutions, and move on. Others snivel and moan, make up off-the-wall excuses to put their weight on somebody else, and try to wiggle out of any situation.

So what if your baby sitter dropped you on your head when you were two; that didn't have *anything* to do with your knocking off a liquor store when you were 22! And it wasn't your girl friend's fault because she wanted some Royal Crown and you didn't have the money. You know how it is; this ducking and dodging could go on forever. Let's get real: you did it because **you chose to!** It may have been a dumb decision, but, by God, your granny didn't do it, **YOU DID!!!**

Don't get caught in the trap of claiming that *whatever* comes down is someone else's fault! This is usually followed by a lot of self-pity, anger, hostility, and endless war talk as you work to sell yourself a world-class lie. Such an attitude is harmful because it keeps you from taking control of your fate and future. Therefore, it is a very powerful trap, in *and* out of the joint. To be free, you must be willing and able to be honest with yourself.

On the other hand, a good attitude is one that looks reality dead in the eye and comes up with positive, constructive steps that lead to progress, achievement, and satisfaction. A good attitude is one that works hard to exercise self-control and accepts the results, good and bad, as your personal property.

A thought to ponder: if you don't accept responsibility for your actions and the results *here and now*, how are you going to control your future? After all, if someone or something else is always ruling your fate, that makes you just a life-long victim of circumstances, politics, luck, the moon, etc. What do you have to gain from being a self-defined puppet?

Cut It All Loose!

> *"Never give up responsibility for yourself to ANYTHING beyond your control!"*

We tend to believe that whatever we need to be free and happy exists *outside of us* waiting to be captured or achieved. We think that if we can only get enough of something or someone, we will be happy. This idea that something outside of ourselves can bring us true satisfaction has one major drawback: **it doesn't work!** People, places, and things outside ourselves can give us pleasure, but they are not the true source of happiness. That is something we must find for ourselves.

It's easy to get hooked on other people or things—especially for prisoners looking for an escape from themselves and the pain and boredom of being locked up. We all know people who have gotten strung out on a variety of drugs, alcohol, risky activities (sticking a gun in somebody's face can be a real rush), or even food. There's nothing like a few Milky Ways to get pumped up for the yard.

Sometimes we want our sweets in human form, so we crave a person. We look up and WHAM, it's love (or lust) at first sight. We kiss, bells ring, and trees burst into bloom in mid-winter. Life is suddenly great. Then, without warning, he/she does an overnight marriage trip to Reno with our best friend, leaving us looking for a strong sheet and a high place to tie it. No good!

What delights us one day often becomes a curse the next. We see this all the time in romantic relationships which self-destruct when one party fails to provide what the other party desires. Jail house romances are especially fragile because they take place long distance, based more on wishful thinking than reality.

Any effort to escape problems or base our happiness on something outside ourselves is just walking on quicksand. No form of pleasure or escape will last forever. After the high comes the letdown, and reality descends on us with a sickening thud. Plus, in the case of addiction, we have the added problem of craving more of the escape mechanism.

In reality, whenever we turn over responsibility for our own life to anything beyond our control, we surrender our freedom and cast ourselves into self-imposed slavery. This doesn't mean that we should avoid loving other people or caring about what happens around us. But we must remember that all persons and things are subject to change. Although we can work to make the odds in our favor, we can't control everything. So we can never have any guarantee that we will get what we want or that things will stay the same. In order to be really free, we must know that we can live and even prosper without the things we desire.

If you can achieve all your desires, that's great. But be prepared to carry on and make the most of your life without them. Have faith in yourself that you can create something worthwhile out of any situation that comes to you. After all, if you can achieve positive results in a prison cell, you can do it anywhere. So quit hanging on to external sources of happiness. *What you need is already within you!* So your next step is to find an effective process of discovery and development.

TAKING ACTION

Planning for Battle

"Preparation is everything!"

FACT: surviving and exiting jail or prison is tough—and that's only half the battle. If you don't stay out, you lose! If the world eats you because you don't know how to cope, you lose!! If you don't make life better than before, you lose!!! Therefore, the better your preparation, the better your odds for being a winner.

Finding your way through the maze takes hard work and great resolve. Every new phase of the journey requires fresh information and re-dedication of your energy, attention, and skill. The first thing you need is a *strategy*. This plan has to be reasonable, workable, and within your ability to complete. Your future success will depend on the quality of your preparation and your personal investment in your plan. As you work to survive and grow, you will need to reshape your thinking (see page 17). The following steps will be helpful as you proceed.

1. Set positive goals—short- and long-term.
2. Make sure they are real—can they be achieved?
3. Check out the risks—is it worth it?
4. Define the steps required—think it all through.
5. Consider what's needed—be realistic.
6. Develop a time table.
7. Collect your resources.
8. Set your priorities and begin with Number 1.
9. Follow through—one step at a time.
10. Be patient and flexible.
11. Give yourself credit as you achieve each step.
12. Celebrate your advances and hang in there!!

Caution: the big trap we all fall into is trying to achieve our long-term goals without dealing with our immediate needs first! We want to achieve too much too soon, so we try to jump ahead, skipping the steps needed here and now. This will defeat our plan, resulting in a lot of frustration and feelings of failure. Success requires the *discipline* to do what needs to be done at the right time. When you get discouraged, review how far you've already come. Sure there's still a lot left to do, but give yourself credit for the progress you've made.

Balance Your Growth

To succeed, there are certain aspects of yourself which only you can explore and develop. By giving attention and energy to each, you grow in many rich and rewarding ways. It's smart to think of each aspect as an essential part of who and what you are. No one of these factors is enough in itself, so don't focus on just one or two that you enjoy or are good at. *The goal is to become a strong blend of all.*

Becoming a "total person" demands work in the following areas. As you develop your plan and strive to better govern your life, you must balance the effort you put into each.

Spiritual Growth

> *"Only by seeking satisfaction and peace within ourselves can we strip our captors of their power."*

Nothing is more essential to our growth than our relationship with our deeper nature and the universe beyond our physical being. Spiritual development helps us find the meaning and purpose of our efforts, develops our inner resources for dealing with problems, gives us a central point of balance, and helps us identify the path which brings the most positive results for ourselves and all around us.

The more aware we are of our spiritual nature, the more progress we will make toward becoming a full and useful person. We must look **WITHIN.** By this I do not mean blind retreat from reality or escape into mental illness. Instead we must focus on and develop our connection with the mystery and wonder of the universe.

There are many religions and spiritual teachings you can follow to develop your spiritual nature. Because this is the most private part of every person, it is not my place to tell anyone what to believe. Each person must look deeply within themselves and within the teachings of any religion or teacher for the path which best leads them toward spiritual advancement. My point is that the development of a balanced person involves spiritual awareness and growth. This critical fact cannot be ignored!

Most religions and spiritual practices offer techniques—such as prayer, meditation, and rituals which celebrate their beliefs—to help people develop spiritual awareness and come into greater harmony with the universe. You can seek guidance from teachers, ministers, or just plain "good people." And regardless of which religion or belief system you follow, you may also wish to learn more about *meditation.*

Meditation is a technique used by many religions and beliefs to promote mental and spiritual development. There are many different methods of meditation. Some teach you to concentrate or focus your mind, while others teach you to free your mind in order to reach beyond your thoughts and get in touch with your spiritual nature. Through this process, you expand your sense of personal control, power, and peace. The advantage of meditation training is that it is something you can do anywhere, without any special equipment, to advance in your religious or spiritual beliefs. This makes it ideal for prisoners who have limits on their resources and physical movements.

I strongly encourage you to *practice daily meditation* as a part of your spiritual development. As with learning to play the piano, dedication and constant practice are the secrets to success. There are a number of good techniques, including Insight Meditation, Anapanasati (Mindfulness of Breathing), basic Zen meditation, and forms of meditation used by Christians and members of other Western religions. No matter what your religious background, you will find meditation concepts and techniques of untold value. Find a method that works for you and *stick with it.* You can refer to **Additional Reading** on page 117 for more in-depth information on how to get started.

Mental Development

"Treat any brain cells you have left like long lost friends!"

Your mind is your greatest single tool for achieving freedom. Before you can begin to be free, you must be mentally clear and honest with yourself, prepared to recognize and cope with reality. Then you can use your mental focus to improve your education, health, job potential, or anything else. No matter how smart you are, you have only been exposed to a tiny fraction of the vast universe of knowledge and skills. Now you have the time to expand and improve your store of knowledge and understanding. Make use of it!

Positive opportunities are scarce in prison, so take advantage of whatever is available. Read, take academic classes and practical training, learn a craft—anything you can find to increase your knowledge and exercise your mind. Find time when you can just *think*, to review and make sense of what you are learning.

Of all the areas of mental growth, *none is* more important than learning to control **ourselves**. What happens in our minds determines how we feel about the world. If we act on our feelings without understanding them or their results, they may lead us into choices based on a mood of the moment rather than sound judgment. A skilled warrior cannot afford to be swayed by fleeting whims! You must learn to master your emotions and the resulting actions.

The best guide is your direct experience. First, watch how your mind and emotions work and how you make decisions. This gives you a chance to identify your values and figure out why you think the way you do. Next observe what actions come from your thoughts and how they affect you and others. Are the results of your behavior pleasant, rewarding, and peaceful? Or do they produce pain, distress, and agitation? Are you making progress in exiting the maze or are you just getting more lost?

When you understand the causes and the effects of your actions, you can choose to redirect your energy toward more positive results. You can use this same process of observation to decide if information and suggestions from other people are accurate and helpful. A big part of growing from a child to an adult is learning to tell who's "right" and what's "real," than adapting to the new information.

As you work to improve your mind, seek out the advice of those who have experience, wisdom, and insight useful to your development. These teachers can help you learn to understand and apply the knowledge you are gaining. Good teachers cannot be judged by what they look like but by what they *know and do*. Don't expect them to be perfect, wear white robes, and float into the room. They are just people who know useful things you can benefit from. In fact, insight often comes in tiny bits from those we least expect as we interact every day.

You may also benefit from studying the teachings of such leaders such as Gandhi, Jesus, the Buddha, Marcus Aurelius, the Dalai Lama, Mohammed, Thomas Aquinas, Malcolm X, Confucius, and others. Often the right thought at the right time helps us break through to a higher level of understanding. Therefore, we must keep our minds and hearts open to wisdom and guidance, *no matter what the source!*

We must remember that our minds are our most powerful tool in the quest for true freedom and a rich, full life. As long as we live, we can continue to develop our understanding and improve the way we think and react to ourselves, to others, and to life itself. By making steady progress in these areas, a person can achieve deep wisdom and peace...in prison and in the free world.

Physical Development

"If you wear out your body, where are you going to live?"

Clearly, if you ignore your body, it will become sickly. On the other hand, the better you respect and care for it, the more energy you have to deal with all aspects of life and yourself. When your body is strong and stable, it acts as a basis for what you do mentally and spiritually.

Although you may not be able to avoid all diseases and accidents, there are two basic factors in physical health where you can take control: your diet and exercise. So consider these basic truths about your body.

1. YOU ARE WHAT YOU EAT.
2. IF YOU DON'T USE IT, YOU LOSE IT. (So exercise!)

First, let's look at what we put in our mouths. One key to good health is to limit the amount of fat, especially saturated fat and cholesterol, in our diets. Saturated fat is found in meat and dairy products but is in a lot of other foods as well. Most Americans consume about 35-40% of their diet as fat. Why? Because it tastes good. But to be healthy, we should have no more than 20-30% of the diet as fat, with less than half of that as saturated fat. Eating too much fat and cholesterol makes us overweight, clogs up our arteries, and causes serious problems. So avoid fat. Eat less red meat and high-fat dairy products; eat more fish and chicken (without skin), skim milk, etc.

The number of calories we take in is another key to a good diet. Calories measure the amount of energy in food. We need the energy, but extra calories make us overweight. And most of the calories in our diet come from fat and sugar. Sugar gives us quick energy and tastes great, but it burns up fast, too. In fact, for a lot of people, sugar is the drug of choice. It gives them a pumped up high, distracts them from their problems, and when the crash comes, they can just pop another Mars bar.

Sugar is high octane fuel, but it doesn't provide the raw materials to build and maintain a healthy body. For that we need protein and complex carbohydrates. Don't think that eating a lot of white bread will take care of this; our body turns refined flour into sugar. So to get healthy, cut way down on sweets and refined carbohydrates (sugar, candy, white flour, honey, etc.) Eat more complex carbohydrates (whole grains, potatoes, fruits, and vegetables). A little book called *The T-Factor* (see **Additional Reading** on page 117) tells you how much fat and calories are in foods.

A big source of sugar in our diet is from sweetened drinks. We drink sodas, tea, coffee, etc., but rarely drink water. The result: our bodies don't function the way they should and the sugar helps make us fat. And we often get a high dose of caffeine, a stimulant drug. Our body's chemistry depends on having enough water in our system—just water, not a combination of drugs and artificial flavorings. To be healthy, you need to drink two quarts of water a day. Cut down on soft drinks, diet drinks, and caffeinated drinks like tea, coffee, and many sodas.

If you want to be healthy, **do it.**

Many of the things we take into our bodies aren't food. We can get hooked on lots of substances that help us pass the time or forget problems, but they definitely aren't good for our bodies or our minds. So give yourself a break: get help to give up smoking, dipping, alcohol, and other addictive drugs. We will discuss recovery from addiction more fully in the section on **Recovery** on page 31.

Also look at *how* you eat. If you stuff yourself at every meal, you will get too many calories. Learn to eat till you're satisfied, then stop. You don't have to clean your plate or finish the bag of cookies at one sitting. There's no sense in skipping a meal to make up for overeating; this will just make you hungrier the next time you eat. Use low-fat foods like fruits and vegetables to fill up before you get to the fats and sweets. And eat slowly; this will help you digest your food better and give your body time to realize it's full.

Now let's look at *exercise.* We used to exercise only to build stronger muscles and burn up excess calories. Now we know that exercise has many other powerful benefits. These extra benefits include:

- Giving you more energy.
- Improving your endurance.
- Maintaining muscles, not flab.
- Increasing the blood chemicals that burn fat.
- Making you feel good by releasing chemicals called endorphines in the brain (a natural high).
- Reducing stress.
- Building self-respect.

So *just keep moving;* it will really improve your health and sense of well-being. Keep one thing in mind: it's not an all or none situation. You cannot change a lifetime of bad habits overnight. And I never said it was going to be easy! Changing your diet and increasing your exercise will take some time. As a prisoner, you can't always control these parts of your life. But you can have some control, such as taking a smaller portion, choosing not to eat some of the less healthy choices, deciding not to pig out on junk foods from the commissary, and working out in your cell.

Become more aware of your health needs and change *what* you can *when* you can. It is up to you to decide what you want and what you're willing to do to feel better and live a richer, fuller, longer life. Changing your eating and exercise habits is a small price to pay to feel good. Get started **today!** It's worth it. And the more you work at it, the easier it will become. You will notice greater overall stability, less depression and anxiety, a more positive outlook, reduced hostility, and increased self-confidence. *You'll feel better,* and that is a real treat inside a prison or on the streets.

Educational Advancement

"You can't dance the Rumba if you don't know the steps!"

As a social outcast, you know what it means to be "powerless." This is not desirable! So when you see *any* chance to improve your ability to function, **grab it.** There is no better way to do this than by improving your education. The better your education, the more you have to draw from as you face the trials and opportunities of life. And the better you can compete in this dog-eat-dog society.

Basic skills—reading, writing, and arithmetic—are essential to employment and just daily living. You may never be a rocket scientist and you may not need a college degree, but you can certainly learn the basics needed to hold a job and understand what is going on in the world around you. If you don't have a high school diploma, you should definitely work to get your GED (high school equivalency diploma). This is something employers look for when screening job applicants.

Don't feel turned off by formal education just because you didn't do well in school when you were younger. As an adult, it is an all new game! You can work on things that interest you and proceed at your own pace. People learn in different ways, so you may need a different teaching approach to help you expand your education. And don't be embarrassed about the things you haven't learned yet. What really counts is how much you are willing to learn from now on. So get off your dead ass, find out what's happening, and get into something interesting and useful. Use your time to improve your mind and skills!

Almost all prisons offer some type of educational program; some provide basic education, while in others you can take college classes. Check with your education department to find out what's offered. If what you want isn't available, try studying what is available. For a prisoner, **any** positive activity is better than nothing. If your education goes beyond the courses provided, you might get a chance to tutor another student; many times teaching is the most powerful form of learning. If there is no education program at all, there may be a staff person or another inmate who would be willing to act as your tutor.

Often inmates are interested in taking correspondence courses. Many of these programs are high quality, but be sure you check on their reputation before you enroll. If you want to use credit from the correspondence course toward a degree, you also need to confirm that other schools will accept those hours. Find out what the joint you're in will permit and look for a staff member to act as your "sponsor" to iron out any problems that come up.

Although basic education programs are often free to prisoners, there is usually a charge for college courses. This can be a real problem for many indigent inmates, but there may be help available. Ask your education department about any free courses or financial aid you might be eligible for. This advice also applies to educational opportunities after release: financial aid is often available, and the school you want to attend should be your best source of information about it. Write to their counseling department for full information and forms. Don't let money stand in the way of your educational progress. Many prisoners and ex-prisoners have attended college thanks to Pell grants offered by the Federal government. These grants have been recently restricted but do your best to qualify.

Vocational Development

"Watching your fingernails grow is NOT a marketable skill!"

FACT: In order to take control and re-build your life, you need a firm desire, the *skill* necessary to make your desire real, the *opportunity* to apply your skills, and *support* from those who can test your plans and assist your efforts.

You won't get anywhere without some job skills: special abilities that allow you to produce something and earn a living. The ability to work to support yourself has a powerful impact on your survival, self-worth, and sense of achievement. These issues are essential for those branded as "outlaws" and are vital to your re-birth after prison.

The goal is to get real good at something people pay money for. Look around; what's happening that you can join in order to increase your skills? It doesn't have to be something you want to do for the rest of your life. Developing a skill helps pass the time in a productive way. Even more important than the skill is the *process of growth* it brings with it!

Find out about any classes or training you can take within the joint. A lot of times you can find a teacher or counselor who will appreciate your initiative and help you. No doubt your options may be very limited, but you don't know if you don't try. If you can get into a trade (for example, welding or sheet metal work) while you are locked up, you can often continue or improve your skills after release. You could try drafting, autobody work, refrigeration repair, accounting, computer science, inventory control, construction—all are worth learning. Training programs in prisons don't always prepare you completely for a job in that field. Some are better than others, but any of them is better than nothing. A wide range of skills may really pay off down the road.

Another area that needs your attention is how to find a job so you can put your skills to use. This is hard for anyone, but it will be a special challenge for you with a criminal record. Remember: preparation is vital to success. The handbook ***Man, I Need a Job!*** (see inside back cover) discusses this issue in depth and offers some practical advice on job hunting and overcoming a criminal record.

Social Growth

"How well you deal with others depends directly on how you deal with yourself!"

We humans are social creatures; a big part of our life involves interacting with others. Think of yourself as one tiny fish in a great big ocean. Alone, you have little power and few resources; it's easy to get eaten by the bigger fish. To survive and prosper, you must learn to swim with the sharks rather than be their dinner. So building good ties with your fellow beings is more than just "good business"; it is essential!

As John Donne said, "No man is an island." To be healthy and whole, we need to learn to see ourselves as connected to other people. We can gain great satisfaction from a sense of closeness to others and a sense of belonging to the family of humankind. The more we grow to view others as "sisters and brothers," the more we can understand about them and ourselves and the more we can share ideas, feelings, and growth. Such a sense of brotherhood is the natural and right way for humans to interact with one another.

But there is a Catch 22 here! We know we need a sense of closeness to help us feel kinship with others. But a prisoner lives with fear, hate, and suspicion of the world around. These negative emotions lead to extreme isolation. In this state of mind, any relationships based on trust, kindness, and compassion are sentenced to a slow but steady death.

CAUTION: this isolation is one of the most dangerous traps in the maze! If you stop and look at it, what greater damage can the experience do than to cut you off from partnership with yourself and with others? By closing your mind and heart, you are in effect exiling yourself to the Island of Total Despair. Isn't this like being in a glass isolation cell, cut off from all that you care about?

The answer is to find a balance point between everything and nothing. While we need a sense of connection with others, all of us will continue to be separate individuals with our own ideas and desires. *Beware of extremes.* Dealing with people doesn't have to be all or nothing. For example, when starting a new relationship, we can find a middle ground between total, immediate surrender and building an impassable wall between ourselves and other people.

It is wise to be careful and selective about whom we deal with and how we interact. For example, a person "shares" different things with a parole officer, a lover, an employer, a minister, a reporter, or a stranger. In every case, it is best to be conservative and develop your relationships slowly based on proven trust. In this way you are not leaving yourself open to hurt, but you are still open to exchanging energy and concern with others. The goal in social dealings is to respond to another person in the way that is most appropriate for your relationship and, at the same time, most beneficial for you and the other person.

Personal Ties

"Relationships are only good when they work."

In order to hold onto some measure of humanity, most prisoners turn to their "people"—those few, if any, who still care if you live or die. Family and friends can become the lifeline to the world, to staying human, to emotional safety, sometimes to hope itself. However, pre-prison relationships change as you and the people you care about adjust to the many burdens of prison life. These relationships will change yet again upon release. Some of the changes are very dramatic (see **Advice for Families** on page 93). As a result, people relate to one another in some strange, intense, and frightening ways. The relationships most often experienced by inmates—and their most common pitfalls—are:

- *Husband/Wife:* Married people often hold onto the past for stability, while trying to build a future based on well-intended illusion. If either or both parties run out of gas, the union can die a painful death. In most cases, this is not anyone's fault, but a natural response to a very unnatural condition. Husbands and wives must find a new way to bond!

- *Man/Woman* (especially jail house romances): Prison romances can get lost in fairy tales and ten-page letters filled with cosmic fantasies. If there is nothing real to stand on when the day of release comes, all hell breaks loose as the parties try to live up to all that Edge of Night stuff.

- *Free World Parent/Inmate Child:* The relationship between parent and child shifts radically from previous patterns but tends to endure better than other relationships. However, some family members may get fed up and turn away, leaving someone else (often the mother) to carry the load. This person may need special help to endure, and the whole family may become bitter and divided over the issue of loyalty to the prisoner.

- *Inmate Parent/Free World Child:* It requires special concern and understanding for a parent in prison to support the growth of his or her children. The child may feel abandoned, fear for the parent's safety, resent authority, do poorly in school, and have many behavior problems. Plus there will be a new set of adjustments to make when the parent is released.

- *Other Family and Friends:* These relationships come and go, depending on how tight the ties are with each individual. Some family members and friends hang in there; others cut you loose like you're ugly and stupid...or they just get tired of the steady effort of letters and visits. It's especially hard for friends to stay close when prisoners go through periods of bitterness and depression.

In every case, changes are so radical that new rules are needed in order to keep love alive. Under these insane conditions, the best way to cope is to work together to re-define and re-direct the ways you deal with one another. You must create a brand-new relationship built on respect and honest concern. Throw out the past, get down to basics, and transform all your relationships into ***true friendship.***

Friendship can occur on many different levels, from someone we see once in a while, to a good long-time buddy, all the way to our closest and most intimate companion. Friendship doesn't necessarily include the passion and intensity we connect with "love," but friendship must be the basis for any loving relationship that lasts over time and is good for both of the loving partners. A good loving relationship is one of the most growth-producing experiences a person can have. Although we usually think of romantic love when we say loving relationship, the relationship between family members, such as parent and child, and between some close friends can also be deeply intimate.

Simply caring strongly about someone, wanting to be together, and wanting that person to care about you is not enough to establish an intimate loving relationship. Love is not just feeling, it is also doing. No matter how much you care about that someone, if your actions are harmful to him or her or block his/her attempts to grow, then you are not truly sharing love.

Therefore, let's review what goes into building a loving relationship that is good for the people in it, providing them valuable closeness along with room to grow. Research has found that the following elements are signs of a positive intimate relationship.

1. *Liking, acceptance, and respect* - Loving partners and friends really enjoy and think highly of each other. They accept each other as they are, even when one makes a mistake. They encourage toward positive goals, rather than nag or criticize. They care about one another's well-being.

2. *Ability to share deep inner feelings* - Partners know it is safe to talk about their most personal feelings, no matter what kind—anger, fear, joy, resentment, or caring. Whatever these feelings, they are acknowledged as being real, even if the other does not agree. The friends accept responsibility for their own feelings, rather than claiming that the other person is responsible for how they feel.

3. *Honest communication* - Partners are willing to tell each other honestly how they feel about any topic. There are no issues that are hidden, off limits, or too scary to discuss. They talk to each other, not about each other.

4. *Balance of closeness and individualism* - Partners respect and encourage each other's differences, without losing their sense of togetherness. No one assumes that they know how the other person feels; each is responsible for knowing and expressing his or her own needs and feelings. The friends are interdependent—they help and support each other, but do not depend on each other as the center of their existence.

5. *Fair balance of power and decision making* - Partners share power and make decisions together, rather than competing to control the relationship. If there is disagreement, they negotiate until they find a compromise.

6. *Effective problem solving* - Partners are willing to admit when they have problems and to work together to solve them. They don't waste time trying to cover up the problem or blame it on each other.

7. *Shared interests and values* - Partners have a core of beliefs, values, commitments, and goals that they hold in common, even while they respect individual differences. They enjoy doing things together.

8. *Flexibility and ability to change* - Partners have common goals, routines, etc., but they are not rigid. They can agree to change plans and head in a different direction without too much stress or discomfort. Their relationship is

not tied to any specific set of circumstances or patterns of behavior.

9. *Openness* - Partners feel comfortable doing things alone or with other people and inviting others into their home and activities. They do not depend on their relationship to meet all of their emotional needs and do not expect each other to give up all outside interests.

In conclusion, a loving relationship is a special and advanced form of friendship. It creates a positive bond between people built on honesty, respect, concern, and common goals. As with the construction of a fine building, the construction of a friendship takes patience, consistency, and determination. Of course, working to build a fresh, healthy relationship will in itself create a lot of stress, so proceed with caution. There are no magic buttons you can push.

One essential ingredient for friendship building is good communication: honesty and openness in expressing how you feel and a sincere willingness to listen when your friend shares feelings with you. Everyone involved must have a strong commitment to the relationship. Otherwise, you won't be willing to spend the time and hard work it will take to make your relationship better. Remember: the main building blocks will be honesty, commitment, communication, and a positive, caring attitude.

Recovery

"Recovery is learning to live in BALANCE!"

From birth to death we face suffering and distress. This is a normal part of being alive. And often we cause greater injury to ourselves by our own choices and behavior. Many of us have developed habits to help us feel better or avoid problems. Unfortunately, some of these ways of thinking and acting make our old problems worse, plus causing new problems. We end up needing more and more of the habit just to stay even, until we lose control of the habit and of ourselves.

These destructive cycles of behavior (addictions) do great damage, robbing us of self-respect and a quality life. By giving something or someone control over our welfare, we set ourselves up for abuse. Surely being in the criminal justice system teaches us that! If we have abandoned control of ourselves to some chemical, person, feeling, concept, or behavior, NOW is the time to grow beyond our addictions. This process of growing beyond past troubles is what we call recovery. Only by growing can we bring joy and balance back into our lives.

The need for recovery is equally great for anyone who has lived through a lot of hurt—whether it came from others or ourselves, from addictions or depression, anger, fear, bad relationships, isolation, prison experiences, or false expectations of ourselves and the world. No matter what the source, most of us carry a whole car load of scars, pain, and emotional garbage that have collected over time. *Now our goal must be to heal.*

The first step toward recovery is to overcome denial and admit that you have a problem. Recovery, like any form of growth, requires commitment and hard,

hard work. No one can do it for you. If you don't think you're ready to pay the price, look at the damage you are suffering by *not* working toward recovery. As long as you're weighed down by past suffering or controlled by addictive behavior, you can never be truly free. So accept it as your responsibility to grow beyond the pain of the past and invest in a positive future. You owe this much to yourself.

Since recovery is such a demanding process, *everyone* needs help along the way. Many wounds are so deep and serious that you just cannot fix them all by yourself. Even Superman needed help when overcome by Kryptonite poisoning. There are many forms of help for recovery in the community: Twelve-Step and other self-help programs, counselors, treatment centers, health departments, hospitals, ministers, friends, and so on.

For prisoners, the choices are much more limited, but even then some kind of help is usually available. Learn to take care of yourself by reaching out for what you need to become a whole person. You can find more information about recovery and finding the right help in the handbook **Life Without a Crutch** (see inside back cover).

While it's totally OK to seek help, the last thing you want to do is transfer your needs and dependent behavior to yet another person or thing! STAY ALERT: no matter what your current status, the final goal is *freedom*. The better you can control your own fate, the better you will feel about everything, especially yourself. The goal is to become your own best friend, to develop your dignity and self-respect. YOU are the foundation of your life and future, no one and nothing else.

Cultural Enrichment

"Knowing your roots helps set the foundation for your future."

You may think of "culture" as going to a dull play or trying to stay awake through an opera. If so, please reconsider. The cultural development I'm talking about is essential to the overall quality of human life. Exploring our culture means developing an understanding of our roots—going back to look at the paths we have followed throughout time and the lessons we have learned. Different societies have unique customs, art, ways of seeing the world and their place in it. More than just social or political history, I'm referring to *all* beliefs and efforts humans have used to make life deeper, richer, and more rewarding.

While being in prison sets you aside from the mainstream of society, it need not cut you off from the rich store of thought and knowledge we have collected over thousands of years. The best of human qualities are captured in art, science, music, literature, poetry, philosophy, religious and creative thought, and so on. No matter what the length of your sentence, you need to be in touch with energy and events from across the world. So reach out. Let your mind expand far beyond the limits of concrete and steel.

Suggestions: use the prison library when and if you can. Read a newspaper to keep up with local and world affairs. Seek out free publications and subscriptions. Have your people send you books on such topics as the history of art, different religions, modern poetry, philosophy, how to draw, primitive cultures, or the customs of other peoples. If you really want to put your time to good use, make an in-depth study of a specific subject, for instance, electronics, a period in history, or cosmology. Or study a foreign country you may want to visit one day; research its customs, history, and current political status. You can even study the language so you will be able to get around and enjoy your travels.

Rather than waste your money on junk from the store, you may buy a subscription to a publication such as **National Geographic**, **The New Yorker**, **Popular Mechanics**, **Time**, **U.S. News and World Report** or whatever excites and expands your cultural horizons. If nothing else, read sections of the library's encyclopedia: *anything* that helps open your mind!

Recreation

"All work and no play makes you a super dull dude!"

The whole trip through the maze is so heavy we tend to focus only on day-to-day survival. This can make life total drudgery. It may sour our outlook on everything and lock us into a cycle of internal misery. We often forget how to laugh and have a good time, although this is essential to our physical and mental health. In truth, one part of growth is play! And it cannot be ignored.

Break out of your depression, get moving, be creative! Go out and play baseball or handball, work on hobby crafts, play checkers, take walks, read light books, watch cartoons—just for the fun of it! This doesn't discount the dreary nature of a pen or the burdens of reconstruction, but you can't afford to get lost in those. No matter how sad your situation, schedule some time every day to lighten up. It doesn't mean you like where you are, only that you have what it takes to adapt and survive.

Such efforts are necessary to keep your stress and attitude under control, both in the joint and with your loved ones. If you build some good "play habits" now, you will find they have a major influence on how well you adjust after release. Having interests to pursue just for fun helps make you a balanced person, as much as any of the issues mentioned above. Allowing yourself this joy in your life becomes your own private reward for taking care of business and doing a good job. It rounds out who you are.

MORE THAN SURVIVAL

"If it can get this bad, it can get this good!"

Life in the system is often an endless series of efforts to cope with crisis. For many, the struggle becomes the focus of every thought and deed. People can get so consumed or obsessed with the daily battle that they lose sight of the positive side of living.

When eaten up with efforts to survive, it's easy to forget there's anything else. You just keep yourself going with dreams of a better life. The danger is that future plans are often just fairy tales you use to retain your hope and courage! When they fall apart, you face even greater failure and disappointment. These pitfalls create a powerful barrier to growth.

To keep from getting lost, you have to remind yourself constantly that there is more to your life than the correctional experience. All your efforts have a positive purpose beyond just making it here and now. They are to prepare you for living a richer, fuller, more satisfying life.

The Bottom Line

Before we begin our journey through the correctional experience, you need to clearly understand: there is SO much *more* to life beyond the criminal justice system! It may not seem that way to you right now; depression and stress can make you lose sight of anything but the madness of the moment. But of all the things necessary for growth, the most essential is to *maintain your hope of future good.*

You must keep your vision focused on the rewards for making it through the maze. So, just for the record, let's ask and answer some basic questions about the reality of the correctional ordeal and why you should bother to seek growth.

- WILL THIS NIGHTMARE EVER END? **YES, absolutely!** One way or another, "this too shall pass." In most cases, it is NOT the end of the world.

- WHAT PRICE HAS TO BE PAID? Honesty, courage, and commitment—absolute determination. The best tools for pulling yourself out of the quicksand are hard work, good choices, patience, and consistency. You must be faithful to your potential as a human being and hold onto your appreciation of the beauty of life.

- WHAT STEPS ARE NEEDED? Establish positive short-term goals and procedures; maintain faith in long-term relief; and pursue growth on every possible level. Work to keep your mind free and your spirit strong. Above all, do not hesitate to seek help! Seek out the wisdom of mature teachers. Search until you find the knowledge, guidance, and support you need. Above all, **never give up!**

- HOW LONG WILL IT TAKE? It takes as long as it takes! That may sound like jive but there is no other honest answer. Many time frames cannot be controlled or predicted, but others (such as the stages of post-release adjustment) *can* be influenced. You can't beat the game totally, but you can get ahead enough to survive. As your strength increases, you will finally find that you have outgrown the past. Although I still struggle to release myself from my past, I know now, without question, that it **is** possible to become a balanced, healthy person! And every day of progress makes tomorrow a bit richer and more exciting, a bit more worth living.

- WHAT IS "SUCCESS" FOR A FELON? It is continued physical freedom, linked with steady progress as a positive, constructive human being. Success is not a constant state, but a state of constant *becoming.* Becoming proud, becoming healthy, becoming vital and free, becoming happy, becoming respected and secure, becoming comfortable, becoming honorable, ***becoming***! It is a condition of slow, steady growth and progress—building more and more control, more and more DIGNITY and PRIDE.

  Success is not what you own but what you ARE. Not the worth of your car, house or bank account, but the worth of your WORD! While others run around playing the fool, hurting themselves and others, you will be a true success because you **insist** on being a person of good heart and sound character. Face reality: success requires a total commitment **while you are still down!** It's not a promise you make to God in solitary, your mamma on Mother's Day, or your mate in a visiting room. It is an absolute commitment to YOU— and you must not betray yourself!!

- CAN IT BE DONE, SHOULD IT BE DONE, AND HOW? Without question, it CAN and SHOULD be done! The main difference between success and failure is a deep-seated commitment to be all that you can be! If there is any one secret to success, it is this: *you have to want it more than anything else in the world!* That means a steady investment of faith and effort. Only absolute dedication will take you far enough.

- IS IT WORTH IT? **Hell, YES...absolutely!** But dealing with the problems a criminal and family must face is tough; you may ask yourself, "What's the use!?" What you're experiencing is so intense that it often seems to overshadow everything else in life. Keep your balance and faith by remembering that this is just one chapter in the book; it is not the book itself!

  Keep your focus: real freedom is the goal! Not some fantasy or Hollywood image, but the real stuff. While others carry their own prison around with them in their heads and hearts, you have the choice of unlocking yourself just a bit more each day. And as you do, you will see more clearly that true freedom can only come from INSIDE of you. This knowledge gives you the power to maintain hope and make good choices, both in the joint **and** in the streets. It is the first step to breaking the chains which bind you!

- THEN WHAT? Is there anything on the other side of this crazy trip?? **The joy of being alive!!** This is a rush which many have yet to truly discover. It **is** worth living for, it **is** worth working for, it *is* worth the price of the ticket!

As we begin our journey through the system together, link what you already know with what you have yet to learn. No matter how much experience you have, search out what you have not yet lived! This will increase your level of freedom and improve the quality of your life. Be of clear mind and strong heart!

WELCOME TO THE MAZE

THE TRIP FROM ARREST TO SUCCESS

"It's sorta like french kissing a water moccasin...it leaves
you breathless and damned relieved when it's over!"

When I caught my first sentence to Angola in 1966 at the tender age of 23, an old con told me that I was caught in a giant maze and no newcomer would know enough to escape it. "Ace," he snickered, "you'll get out when you've learned enough, and in your case that's gonna take a long time!" Regrettably, he was right. Here I am, 26 years later, still struggling to understand and overcome what began as an act of violent passion so long ago.

Like most, I hit the joint frightened but determined to handle whatever came down. I quickly found that even the most street-smart person in the world isn't ready for all the sick jive that comes with being "Property of the State." Sure, most people learn to survive, but there is no joy in just living from hour to hour like a monkey in a cage. In the end, you find that no matter how much you've been around, your insight only scratches the surface of what you need to lead a truly *quality* life.

Since 1977 I've worked with over 20,000 ex-cons and have been amazed to find how similar our problems and needs are. In fact, it is the **predictable nature** of the whole trip which makes this book possible. I have also learned that there is a *beginning* and an *end* to this wild race, with a whole bunch of vicious twists and turns in between. The more you know about how to bank a turn, the greater your chances of still being right side up at the end of the run.

Let me be right up front with you. If you have been out of the criminal justice system ten years, have a solid life and loving friends, a rewarding job and stable income, personal security, pride in your achievements, and peace of mind, you don't need this book. But, if you have **anything less** than the above, be honest with yourself and accept that you still have a LONG WAY TO GO.

A Down and Dirty Tour

"Walk slow and drink a lot of water."

The goal of **Maze** so far has been to help remove the blindfolds so we can stop stumbling in the dark and reliving the same traps and dead ends time after time. Now, with better vision, we will pursue the secrets that lead to final exit and life beyond this puzzle.

To do so, we're going to visit the major danger zones together, step-by-step, from arrest to recovery five years after release. The focus will NOT be on legal issues but on the mental and social changes needed to survive and get ahead of this ugly game. Such a trek covers a LOT of ground so it will be a *down and dirty tour*, with only minutes spent on what often takes years. Our goal is to offer an honest and useful guide that will improve a person's chances of living through and beyond this mad journey.

You may be a "state-raised" character or some careless square who just drove up. Or you may be a family member of a prisoner or perhaps a student in search of knowledge. You may know a little or you may know a lot about the path, but never think for a heartbeat that you know it all. No matter how hip, hard-core, or get-down you may be, this blue print contains areas you have yet to explore and conquer! Why spend 25 years of hard knocks, panic, and pain just to discover what you're already holding in your hands?

For their own sanity and safety, loved ones should give special note to the last chapter **Advice for Families of Offenders** on page 93. Its practical insight will help family members survive and grow beyond this painful period in their lives. This section also offers prisoners an honest picture of what their people are faced with and what it takes for them to handle grief, fear, and depression. The more an inmate knows about the plight of loved ones, the better he or she can support and encourage them during their times of critical need. Never forget that it's a two-way street!

The magic of this map is that it helps you soar above the limits of mere day-to-day survival. It offers you "the big picture"! Here is a bird's eye view that you'll never learn just standing on the ground. But to tap its power, don't just skip around—**READ IT ALL.** Think about it, step by step. And then go back and read it again: especially the parts you've yet to live. This is the only way you can grasp the journey as a **whole** rather than getting lost in a series of remote events. If you reflect on what you learn here, you will come away with priceless insight into the plight of criminal justice "travelers." Although following this road brings danger, damage, and dread, we are going to regard it as a *useful challenge and a chance to grow.*

WAKING UP IN A CAGE: ARREST TO CONVICTION

YOU'RE BUSTED, SUCKER!!!

"Falling off into the criminal justice system is like being struck by lightning—-right on top of your old bald head!!"

Arrest is the first step into the alien world of the American system of justice. It can be just a short-term hassle or the start of a long, painful journey that deeply affects someone's life for years to come.

It's a total shock to awaken in a jail cell, alone and confused in a world based on brute force, mind games, endless deceit, and frantic hopes for release. A family member or loved one is *equally* stunned by a prisoner's 3 a.m. call from a jail pleading for help.

An arrest upsets a person's balance and sense of security. It explodes patterns of living that you're used to. Immediately you snap to the fact that you are helpless and have no control over your freedom. Time seems to stop as your contact with the world is suddenly cut off.

The first concern is making bail because there isn't much you can do to aid your case from inside a cage. So you reach out to *anyone* who will respond: to those few folks, if any, who care and will up your bond. Thus your arrest disrupts the lives of loved ones and friends who are called on to provide money and support.

It can also affect your relations with friends, your boss, school, and many others. The results of this abrupt event can pass in a matter of weeks or be the start of years of isolation and heartache. The longer someone walks this trail of tears, the more intense and far-reaching the effects.

LONG WALK OFF A SHORT PIER

"Sick, helpless feelings come over you like a black cloud blotting out the sun."

As you move deeper into the maze of police, lawyers, jails, courts, and prisons, some heavy social and mental changes occur. Without warning, things turn up side down and inside out. For both the "citizen accused" and loved ones, parts of daily life are severely disturbed.

To cope with the insanity of jail and the mystery of the courts, you frantically search for a "good" lawyer who will perform a legal miracle and remove this threat to your welfare. You lose lots of sleep over what the D.A. is going to do, what your probation or parole officer is going to do, what your mother or wife is going to do, what your lawyer is going to do, ETC. Your mind is filled with anxiety and dread. Should you cop out or go to trial, does your family still support you, can you handle the warfare inside a prison, will your girl friend wait if you catch ten years, and so on. **NOBODY** wants to believe they are going to be found guilty or be sent to prison, and neither nor do the folks who care about them.

Here is where you learn that justice is often linked to the size of your wallet and that the lawyer you want is the one you cannot afford. Many folks end up with a court-appointed attorney, who is far too busy to talk with you until ten minutes before court. In the meantime, *everyone* hopes to slide with a probation or short sentence, but too often it doesn't work. There is NO promise of sanity or reason in the extreme forces which command a person's fate at this point.

It's impossible to outguess the system: it's a brainless business that defies prediction. Things get so crazy and stressed out that many people end up plea bargaining just to end the immediate madness. In fact, *many* pressures are brought into play to drive you to cop a plea that will keep the wheels of justice rolling right along. For the accused and family, this is a time of hell on earth.

It is also a critical turning point that often ends in life-long damage and hard feelings. Many of the people who will read this book got done in right about here. Just before my hearing, my lawyer went into the men's room in the Federal courthouse and shot up white china junk he'd scored with money he beat my mother for. I guess he needed a fix of courage to plead me guilty for the max. "Justice" is a seven letter word; so is "goodbye."

WITH ONE FALL OF THE GAVEL

"Son, how old are you?" "23, your Honor." "Just entering the prime of life...and I'm going to take seven years of it. Seven years hard labor, Angola State Penitentiary. Next case."

Lost in a fog of confusion, the hour of sentencing arrives—a moment of shock and dismay for both the prisoner and loved ones. Standing before the judge, a few magic words and, **BINGO**, you belong to the State. Even when you know what's coming down, you're too spaced out to grasp what's happening or how it will affect your future.

It all happens so quickly! The gavel falls and the deal is done. There is no going back. If your sentence results in jail time, a probation, and/or a fine, you can usually cope with it without too much trouble. Jail time may be fairly short, and probation requirements are usually not *too* heavy: you must report, follow the rules, and pay your fees. It definitely can be tough, but if you keep your life halfway together everything turns out OK. 90% of probation officers' time is spent on the 10% of their case loads who just *insist* on going to the pen.

Many probationers feel very abused by the actions of the police and courts.

It's human nature to promise *anything* to keep from going down and then bitch and moan after the deal is cut. People often show their anger and distress by resisting their terms of probation. Some get so hostile they say to hell with it and fail to report. This can happen when people get depressed, careless, lost in addiction, or sideways with their probation officer. Yet no matter how absurd being on probation can get, it is **far** better than going to the pen! To make it on probation, you need to stay cool and clean, keep your act tight, and meet your commitments. There will still be unexpected dangers, but if you are on top of your game, you have a good chance of success.

SIGN ME UP!

"If you sign up and don't show up, lean way over and kiss your ass goodbye."

When push comes to shove, most people would rather be eaten by fire ants than go to the joint. So they rush to sign up for any local program that will satisfy the judge and keep them out of prison. But this can be a real trap when it turns out to be a bumpy ride!

No matter what kind of program you join or get assigned to, it will have its rules and requirements that cut into your life, demanding your time, energy, and resources. Even more, your probation officer will expect to see **positive changes** in your attitude and actions. So just because you score work release, boot camp, drug treatment, electronic monitoring, sex therapy, family counseling, a halfway house, etc., you are not home free. Stay alert: if you drop the ball, the judge will slam dunk you!

You are at a point where you have an important chance to work your way out of the maze and avoid the much heavier changes down the road. The requirements may seem Mickey Mouse, but do yourself a favor and take them seriously. One thing for a probationer (and parolee as well) to keep in mind: about *half* of all people sent to the joint were under supervision on the streets and failed to comply with the contract they signed. In many cases, revocation comes from walking away from a program or just failing to report, even if you don't pick up a new felony.

So if you are sentenced to probation or put in a program as an alternative to prison, make the best of a bad situation. Be very careful not to send *yourself* down the river. If you do, you'll find yourself chained to someone even uglier than you, on a bus that doesn't stop at the Dairy Queen.

FLUSHED AND FORGOTTEN

"The day you're sent to prison, listen for the sound of running water because you've just been flushed down the social toilet!!"

If the sentence is to prison, everything gets radical! One minute a citizen with rights, the next just a slave with a number for a name. Ownership of you is transferred to the State. If you want to do *anything* from now on, a stranger with a bad attitude has to give you permission. In truth, this is one of the most dramatic and far-reaching moments a person can experience. It's odd how something which takes only ten minutes in court can require ten years of supreme madness to deal with and another ten years of stress and hard work to recover from.

The prisoner and loved ones turn to the lawyer for guidance about an appeal, shock probation, boot camps, visiting hours, what can be taken to prison, how parole works, etc. But the lawyer is **long gone**! The family then turns to the prisoner for direction, but he or she doesn't know what's happening either. It's the blind leading the blind!

This new part of the journey may last a few months, twenty years, or even unto death; it often demands every last resource of a person's mind, body, and spirit. Indeed, every day can bring new problems and heartache. Few experiences in our culture present a greater demand for change or a more intense challenge for personal growth. As I was told, "It's a short step down and a long step up."

If sentenced to prison, especially for a long period, you cease to be part of the real world. You become a mere ghost that walks and talks, a faceless number. Overnight all contact with life as you know it—food, fashions, daily activities, *everything*—comes to a screeching halt. Once sentenced to the joint, you become a public zombie, physically alive but as socially dead as a door knob.

You have just bought your ticket to the maze. The door marked "IN" is lit in neon; you even get an armed escort to help you enter. But once inside, you are stone alone and there is no exit in sight. Your thoughts, feelings, dreams, ambitions, skills, and hopes suddenly cease to be important to **anyone** but you and those few who choose to stand by you. From this point on you will be constantly looking for a way out. But what appears to be an "Exit" often turns out to be only a door painted on a concrete wall!

SAYING GOODBYE

"It's hard to say a tender goodbye as you're being dragged away in chains."

Sudden loss of physical freedom is shocking. But the hardest part is being cut off from those you love. In many cases everyone's attention has been focused on the plea bargaining or trial. All energy has been spent on the outcome of efforts in court. As a result, there is seldom any real chance to prepare emotionally for the impact of separation.

By now everyone is so blown away and things move so quickly that there may not be any real chance to say goodbye. This is especially true for children; they are deeply confused by the stress and excitement and are trying to deal with the fact that daddy or mommy has vanished. This places a heavy burden on the person who is caring for the kids, answering their questions, and filling the gap of the parent's absence.

If you are on the streets and know what's coming, call time out a few days before you are to be sentenced or report to prison. If you can, it's good to spend some quiet, quality time with those you love, just being close and trying to calm down. It helps to build some happy, positive memories to fall back on later.

I don't know of any graceful or easy way to cope with tearful farewells. Everyone involved, prisoner and family, reflects on what they wish they had said and done when they still had the chance. If the separation was rude and abrupt, it is important that the prisoner get in touch with the family as soon as possible and assure them of his or her safety and well being. There is no reason to burden them with horror stories or to unload a lot of emotional garbage on them which they have no way to remedy.

Now the whole nature of how people relate to each other changes. The day-to-day chance to talk, share, and touch comes to an abrupt end and new ways must be found. From now on you must learn to express yourself in letters, cards, poems, art, and visits. Your contact becomes *indirect*, but you can learn to adjust and find creative ways to express your thoughts and feelings. For more insight into these changes, give special attention to **Advice for Families** on page 93.

I'M GONNA APPEAL!

"Don't panic and base your future on an endless series of false hopes; stay calm as a clam and get the facts!"

A person just convicted almost automatically considers an appeal. This often occurs because the decisions of the court are considered "unfair." Yet fairness, in the sense of moral correctness or justice, has even less to do with the appeal than it did with the trial.

Before you do anything, TWO facts have to be dealt with. First, if you plead guilty, generally no pre-trial motions and little evidence was presented. Agreed pleas are not heard by a jury and involve no jury charge. Therefore, there is very little to appeal from a guilty plea. Guilty pleas are rarely set aside on appeal.

Second, appeals are not a chance to have someone else correct a sentence or make a "fair" ruling. Instead they are simply motions which tell a higher court that someone—judge, juror, or attorney—made a **big** mistake. An appeal is not a new trial. It is a *written request to review one or more specific legal decisions* made during the case. Only those trials where a big mistake was made will be reversed (when the Court of Appeals finds some error in the trial court's actions and orders a new trial or a dismissal).

More than nine out of ten appeals will be affirmed (left unchanged). In the meantime, the appellant (defendant who appeals the case) and his or her loved ones can become absorbed in a long, expensive (many years and many thousands of dollars) process that may only build false hopes.

Appeals take a long time, partly because so many are filed. The frivolous (worthless) ones stand in line with the good ones. The appellant spends valuable time and funds in a process that is unrewarding 90% of the time. So before you jump off into it, you need to take a close look at the appeals process and the facts of your case.

This requires a review of the transcripts (official record) of the trial. These are the first major expense: about $1,500 for a three-day trial (unless you qualify as indigent). Then you need a *qualified* appellate lawyer to closely review the proceedings to see if some major mistake was made in the process of the trial (usually requires a retainer, and much more if the lawyer decides to take the case). Remember, you must find a mistake in the *process*, not in the facts. If none exists, you have no basis for an appeal and that's that. Cold but true.

If you have a short sentence, it may not make sense to appeal because you may make parole or be released before the appeal is finally heard. But for someone with heavy time *and* serious trial errors, it may be real smart to learn some law and fight your case. There are a lot of jail house lawyers who will claim special insight into how to beat your case, but very few really know their business.

Like anything else, the quality of your efforts and preparation are *critical*. Be careful not to let your despair warp your judgment. If you're going to do it, spend the time and energy to do it right. Take things one step at a time, learn patience, and don't send your mother out to mortgage her home to fund some hopeless grasp for freedom.

THE CORRECTIONAL EXPERIENCE

FALLING OFF INTO HELL: LIFE IN PRISON

CHAINED DOWN AND PRISON BOUND

Stripped and Shipped

*"I was no longer a 'citizen,' just a social outcast—so much
trash exiled to a giant, government-run dumpster."*

They always pull the chain before the birds get up, so you begin your day locked down inside a crowded, smelly old bus or hunched over in the back of some sheriff's van. Of all the trips a person takes during a lifetime, few if any have such a powerful outcome! While the traffic moving around you rushes toward work and school, you struggle with your chains, listen to the drum of the engine, and fight to control the knot of sick fear growing in your guts.

As the miles click by, an amazing mutation is taking place. You *know* something very heavy is happening but cannot grasp the nature and impact of it all. In fact, you are not moving from "point to point" like the rest of the traffic, but from one dimension of reality to another. Later in life you may try to explain to others the shift that occurred during those dawn hours, but only those who have made this unearthly journey will ever understand.

Like a snake shedding its skin, your identity starts to peel away. Rather than being a parent, student, or truck driver, the label of "**criminal**" begins to define you. Over the months and years to come, you will grow to identify with and adapt to your new role. From this day onward, your attitude toward yourself and the world will change, and so will the way you carry yourself. It's not unusual for every aspect of the way you think, feel, and behave to be touched by your new status.

By the time you finally arrive, all stiff and frantic, the early changes have already occurred. Whatever your social status when you got aboard, it now resides in the weeds along some blacktop highway. Every newcomer feels buck naked, like prime vulture bait. And from this heartbeat on, 90% of your time and energy is spent working to cover your ass. It is this **constant**, **urgent demand** to adapt or perish which draws you, against your will, into the Devil's Den.

Welcome to Hell

Going to prison is like waking up one morning in the twilight zone. Everything may seem the same but in fact everything is different. What "appears" is often not what actually exists. Different values and rules are now in force. But forget the war stories; what's the bottom line? What is a prison *really* like? Not the walls, the bunks, and the bars, but the life lived inside?

I've heard it defined many ways. "A concrete graveyard," "a human outhouse," "a hate factory," just to name a few. In truth prison is a huge pressure cooker filled with human pain and treachery, all mixed together and simmering on a slow fire of stress and fear. No matter what words you use to describe it, it is a place where people silently cry in their sleep and fight to hold onto their sanity and hope.

Prison is not **real** in the way things are on the streets. But it's such a hard, cold, painful illusion that it seems to be reality-for-sure! Actually it's a false image, a *cruel cartoon*. It doesn't run by the same rules as the world you've left or the one you'll return to. There is no "long-term" or "short-term"—there is only **right here, right now!**

Like a computer, what makes a prison work is its *operating system:* the way people and things are defined and set up to relate to one another. First, the Cons to the Man and the Man to the Cons. Then the Man to each other and the Cons to each other. And, last, how everybody handles their roles and business, day in and day out. When you learn how things really come down, you begin to see that ALL the players are acting out jive roles—roles which are totally opposite to successful life on the streets. And I mean BOTH the rulers and the ruled!

The number one prison code is that "kindness is weakness." **Everyone** wears "a different face for every place" and preys on one another, with mental and physical backstabbing being a daily reality. *Quickly* a prisoner learns that it's your "friends" who can hurt you the most. Only those close to you *know* where you keep your property and how to jack with your mind when your mate doesn't write. This is a place where screwing with the minds and emotions of "gofers" is considered good sport. So, in the end, you cannot afford to have friends as they exist in the streets. You may go through a series of running buddies or folks you hang out with, but you rarely let anyone get close to your heart. This makes a person very alone and at odds with the whole concrete jungle.

You soon discover that prison is a phony, lonely place. It's *painfully easy* to get tricked or trapped into living by terror, pressure, and unending hustles. For many it becomes a mad house where nothing makes sense, a void where nothing matters but survival. One major step in survival is understanding the nature of **respect**: learning how to give it and how to get it. Respect is based on the size of your heart and how you carry yourself; it is not built on the size of your arms or mouth.

Dancing Through a Mine Field

> *"It's like stepping off into a mine field. You never know when the next blast will come, without warning, totally beyond your control."*

A prison is like a giant trash can occupied by 3,000 hungry, hostile cats **all** after one little fish bone! In order to survive, you must learn the rules and adapt in a hurry. If you don't, you perish.

There are no true signposts to reality in prison, so it's easy to get lost if you don't run a tight ship. Many people do their time lost in a fantasy world, placing faith in what they wish could be (like bogus writs, pending changes in the law, early release, another appeal, etc.) rather than what actually is. Also, many inmates *and* their loved ones get lost in the mindless jive of prison war and power games. This is deadly because each new day draws them deeper into the false-hood and deceit of prison life.

Usually there are no logical reasons for things that happen in prison. Life is a roller coaster moving from one crisis to another, with sheer boredom filling in between the stops. Everyone who takes this trip—inmates and families alike—has to cope with a series of abrupt, absurd events. It's usually a waste of time to try to figure out what has come down or why. Most of the time it's better for an inmate and loved ones to focus on *damage control* rather than going into blind battle.

I admit that it is *very* hard not to react emotionally and violently when some-thing "totally wrong" comes down. You want to stand up for yourself and release your anger and frustration. Such reactions are very human but ask yourself one question: "Is this going to make things better for me or make things worse?" If the answer comes back, "Worse—but I don't give a damn," then you are playing right into the hands of the enemy. Stop. THINK. And refuse to go for the bait!

Beware the Traps

> *"It's an endless series of trap doors. You never know which*
> *one is going to drop open or when, so you've always got to*
> *be on your toes."*

From the moment you enter the maze to the moment you leave, you must expect to deal with countless traps. Like a human Nintendo game, each step deeper into the system presents a new set of dangers.

The good news is that you can learn to cope by basing your reactions on smart mental choices rather than raw emotions. You must learn to survive and flow with what comes down around you. This involves two levels of skill. First, you must learn to control your *mind and emotions*, as discussed in **Reshape Your Thinking** on page 17. The second is covered in the following chapters dealing with physical and practical adjustments. As you learn to merge both types of skills, your present and future welfare will continue to improve.

If you keep to yourself, think before you act, watch what's going on, stay alert, and keep your mouth shut, you can do your time without always being on someone's hit list. NOTE: do NOT accept favors; the payback is often more than you can afford. Staying invisible is the best way to go! Obviously, **anything** that makes you a target is uncool. The basic traps to avoid are drugs, gangs, sex, and gambling. I would include coping with the crazies and the fools in that list, but they come with the territory. You have to learn to be *political* and deal with the snitches and idiots as smoothly as possible.

How you carry yourself and deal with people controls your fate! Rip offs finally get ripped off. Con men end up getting chumped. What goes around comes around. Lots of people fall off into gangs in the joint for protection, dealing, status, etc. But it is usually a bitter trap! All it did for Jesse James was get him shot in the back by a cowardly "home boy." Even Jesus got done in by one of his tight men for a handful of silver. Watch those around you very carefully: if they will backstab someone else, they will sure as hell do it to you. So stay alert to reality! When your fate can be swayed by a bunch of self-serving predators, it's amazing how quickly you can become the next in line to be had.

To put it bluntly, this is not a make-believe game where you can call "King's X." It is a cold-blooded horror show where your decisions and actions *directly* impact your stark survival. Therefore, the **last** thing you want to do is to surrender control of yourself to a set of rules made by losers, liars, and mental retards. That's the most honest way I know to put it.

No matter how careful you are, there's no guarantee that trouble won't find you from time to time. But life is a lot easier if you focus on reality and don't beat on your chest, run your head, or try to abuse those weaker than you. This is just smart business, because there will always be someone close at hand to do the same unto you.

Here are some basic rules to follow to help reduce the hassles:

- ALWAYS think before you act; afterwards is too late.
- Trust no one and be very cautious who, if anybody, you pick as friends.
- Live your life in prison, not in fantasies of the streets.
- Maintain your sexual dignity by **any** means necessary.
- Hope for the best but expect the worst.
- Obey the rules...no one said you have to like it.
- Never put your business on the street or wave any flags.
- Treat your loved ones like 24-karat gold.
- Ask for only what you *need to survive.* Make no demands and don't snivel.
- Get healthy and stay strong: physically, mentally, and emotionally.
- Keep your head down and your mouth shut until you learn the game.
- Do unto others *just the way* you want them to do unto you!
- Respect yourself: never surrender your mind, body, or soul.
- Refuse to engage in self-pity.
- Stay calm as a clam and patient as a saint.
- Be real: the only thing you run in prison is your head.
- Never try to beat a shark at his own game. Sharks never sleep.
- Hear no evil, see no evil, and, for your own sake, speak no evil!
- Don't accept favors, gamble, borrow money, or push drugs.

- Never play tush hog, bad ass, or King Kong: you will be killed.

- AIDS leaves no survivors: masturbate.

- The past is dead and stinking: move forward, never backward.

- Grow! Use your time to expand your knowledge and understanding.

- Avoid prison mind games! Do your time, don't let it do you!

- Don't try to pray your way out.

- Get and stay real with yourself: live on facts, not illusions.

- Figure out who put you in the joint: look in the mirror.

- Do your own time, quietly and with class.

- Prepare yourself for where you want to be three years after release.

- Help others when you can, but don't be a chump.

- Do square business: earn respect.

- Leave your anger in the joint when you walk out.

- Keep this book handy and review it every three months. Tell your people to get a copy; it will improve their understanding.

Reading the Signs

"Knowing when to duck is very valuable information!"

Adjusting to all these new "rules of the game" can be overwhelming. But there is one powerful secret that the Man never tells you and your mother doesn't know. *Everything* that happens to you is part of a ***predictable*** pattern. What you are feeling and living through has been repeated time and time again since the first U.S. jail opened in 1789. The boxes have different names, but what goes on inside of them is all the same.

As one isolated person, you feel helpless against the forces which confront you. It is natural to believe that what's coming down is unique to *you and you alone.* NOT SO! Millions of people from coast to coast are, will, or have walked the same path, felt the same feelings, and shared the same hopes as you are this moment! I promise you this is true.

So how does this help you? It is your first essential tool for survival and growth. It means that adjustment into **and** out of prison happens in some highly predictable stages, most of which can be forecast like a pending storm. In short, you can learn to prepare for events and your own reactions before they happen. You are **not** totally powerless and at the mercy of the situation!

Stay alert! Watch the changes that others go through; look for patterns in their actions and reactions. Become aware of the stages of your own changes and behavior. For the first 90 days you are numb with shock and confusion. During this time you're tested in a dozen different ways; you may have to go into physical battle to keep your dignity. No matter who you are, this is a hard period filled with distress. After the initial shock come six to nine months of grief and depression from losing your freedom and family. Most people do tough time during this period and have to be very careful not to lose their balance. To make things worse, you must carry this burden in silence; if you "snivel," it is taken as a sign of weakness by others.

Some young first offenders are sent to a boot camp for a short sentence. In this case, you're busy from the moment you arrive. You don't have time to get used to anything because you're not there long enough for your finger prints to dry. Boot camps are like military basic training and are run for shock value. You're supposed to toe the line after you see what it's like to be dragged off to the joint in chains. If you happen to get into a boot camp, keep a low profile, follow the rules, and don't blow it.

However, most people who have been down before or who drive up with a heavy load do their time the old-fashioned way: sunrise to sunset behind brick walls, double fences, and rows of shiny razor wire. It takes about 12 to 24 months to really settle in and get a grip on yourself. By the third year you have a good handle on what's cooking throughout the joint. By the fifth year, you've found a "home." From then on it's a matter of keeping a handle on what you've been able to carve out for yourself. Be careful—folks get **VERY** protective of their turf!

While you are learning to cope with what's going on around you, another very important change takes place. You slowly adjust to the way time *itself* changes. A day in a cage is like a week in the free world, a week like a month, a month like a year, a year like a decade. And as for holidays, well, they are just another day—one less to do. Events seem to stretch out as daily life goes into slow motion! If you do three to five years or more, you will definitely notice the impact of this time shift during your first six months of life on the streets!

All the changes you go through have deep and long-lasting effects both during and after captivity. Little by little, day by day, you adapt to the folly of a joint in order to handle it. As you become more and more cut off from *everything* you value, the warm, positive aspects of daily life slowly drift away. At the same time you become more and more involved with the cut-throat values of prison life.

So stay aware! After a few years, contact with the real world slowly dies and memories grow dim. Then it's all too easy to get lost in the false, shallow trash that goes on 24 hours a day. After five to seven years of this, you can get so caught up in prison values that you become more of a *prisoner* than a *person*. At this point, you have become "institutionalized"—mentally more "in than out."

If this happens it is because you have simply run out of gas; the joint has drawn off all your energy and hope. As a cell partner once put it, "You can't see over the barbed wire anymore." No matter how much time you are doing or under what conditions, you must not let this happen! The only time you're **really** beat is when you surrender your spirit to the falsehood and dishonor of a prison. Hold on to your self. And **never** lose sight of your need for constant growth as a human being.

STAYING IN TOUCH WITH THE WORLD

Misery Loves Company

> *"The world views you as they do atomic waste. If you have a faithful friend or devoted mother left, treat them like 24-karat gold. It's loving, it's right—and it's good business."*

Prison is often referred to as a war zone. And in war, people must work to hold onto their humanity and the values that make life worth living. Most often we do this through our ties with family, loved ones, and friends. However, prison life can cause serious damage to our relationships with our people in the free world.

FACT: Inmates are often very selfish, demanding a lot from their people. Partly this is because we are cut off from the world. As prisoners, our status is so harsh and remote that we have little to hold onto and many limits on what we can do for ourselves. So we tend to overwork those few who care. The most obvious way is for money: for store goods, visits, appeals lawyers, phone calls, a radio or fan for our cell, law books from the free world, support for children, new tennis shoes for the rec yard, etc.

Inmates are often equally thoughtless of their loved ones' limited time, energy, and emotional well being. We act as though they have nothing else to do but react to our needs and requests. How dare they go on living day to day while we suffer in the joint! When we get ourselves into trouble, we tend to expect everyone around us to pay the price. Being in prison makes it easy to get lost in wishful thinking, self-pity, and false ideas, so let's set the record straight.

Fact One: In many cases your people are poor, physically ill, and emotionally beat all to hell. They often try to keep this to themselves so as not to burden you. In fact there is damn little they can do, if anything. They are not miracle workers. And don't cop an attitude because they all get together for Christmas dinner and actually have a good time!! Do NOT lay guilt trips on people for going to see a Walt Disney movie while you're stuck in an isolation cell.

Fact Two: Your old lady is NOT sleeping with the 5th Army! Just because you're scared and insecure, don't expect her to sit in a corner and cry till you get home. She needs your trust and day-to-day support to be well and strong. It's bad enough that you are a social zombie who comes alive only in loud visiting rooms, long letters, and sexual fantasies. Show her what true love is by being fair, honest, considerate, and trusting. This may not work; you might break up anyway. But I guarantee that you stand the best chance of keeping her if you are a true friend and concerned partner.

Fact Three: Only in very rare cases did your people have anything to do with why you are in the pen. You are there because you got "loose and ludicrous," in one way or another. Even if it was a bum rap, it is still YOUR bum rap. So in most cases your people are having to deal as best they can with a condition you and the State laid on them. In short, it's your load to carry. When you need serious help, make sure what you ask for is fair and doable. Don't send your pregnant wife to see the judge or ask your blind mamma to put up her retirement money for your appeals lawyer. Come on!

Fact Four: Loved ones are the only "safe" people on whom you can unload your feelings; this includes your fears, anger, war talk, anxiety, and distress. They are the only people you can afford to be human with. But what do you think it does to your mother's mind to tell her you want to kill your cell partner for stealing your cigarettes? It is understandable that you are upset but, for God's sake, cut her some slack!! If you don't know how to handle the madness of your situation, what makes you think she does?

Fact Five: As a "criminal" you don't have many friends left. And even they are two-thirds fed up with your status *and* your jive. Many inmates have burned their people really badly, left them hanging, and after all this, can't understand why their folks don't trust and support them. So you want to walk real light with those few friends and loved ones who still care about you. Be careful not to get so angry and depressed you drive them off! And, last, don't take anything for granted: express your sincere appreciation for *every* positive effort and favor they do.

First Your Money...

> *"There's an old jail house saying: 'First your money, then your clothes, then your old lady/man goes'."*

No inmate in the world wants to hear that! It's bad enough being powerless, cut off from the community, and fighting for your survival without having to worry about losing your main squeeze. For most prisoners, the most important part of their personal life is that person dearest to their hearts.

Yet the loss of important personal ties in prison is a frequent and painful fact of life. It does no good to deny the reality of it or to sit around and be eaten up by fear and worry. It is **critical** to keep your mental and emotional balance! We all have to live through deaths in the family, and they can take place on many levels. If your relation with someone dear to you hits the wall, you cannot afford to be overcome by grief and depression. If you're not real careful your grief will come out in anger and violence, which usually makes your plight even worse. *Never* permit the agony that comes with loss of a loved one to blind you. **Beware:** your position doesn't permit you to surrender to grief.

To make things worse, we often make up a lot of stuff in our minds that just isn't true. This happens because we lose track of reality, get lost in self-pity, are overcome by fear, or at times just go totally insane. For example, a friendship that was only a passing thought on the streets becomes a flaming inferno right off *The Young and the Restless* when you catch a fresh ten-year sentence! Why?

Because you need something to hold onto. But just because you need it doesn't make it real. The problem with make-believe is the pain you get when reality kicks you dead in the middle of your chest! So don't set yourself up for more distress than you've already got. In the end, the hope and support you hunger for has to be found WITHIN YOU.

Even though it's a major relief to have somebody out there, what if he or she just cannot hang on? I'm not talking about a worthless person here, but one who is *simply overwhelmed.* Remember that prison and its effects on people are totally unnatural. There isn't any guaranteed way to keep a romance or marriage alive under such absurd conditions. Many try, and really give it their best shot, only to find it's just too crazy and painful to handle.

Inmates cope with their fear of lost loves in different ways. Many prisoners try to direct or dominate the life of someone in the streets. They use pitiful stories, guilt trips, spiritual awakenings, romantic promises, vows of long overdue change, or even threats of bodily injury. This is mostly to give themselves the illusion of retaining some of the security and control they have lost as a prisoner. The person in the free world may even try to go along with the game, but it is Grade A jive! No one can or should "possess" or rule another, *especially* from the third tier of a cell block.

The only *real and useful way* to build or maintain a personal bond from inside a prison is through honesty, respect, and true concern. In fact, this genuine caring is all that really works on the streets, too. Do yourself a big favor: forget the fantasy/romance trip, and focus totally on **true friendship**! It's the only way to keep love alive in the face of loneliness, midnight anxiety, holiday depression, fear of abandonment, the screaming hornies, visiting room heartache, and the endless forms of confusion, longing, and pain.

Building positive, rewarding friendships is an art in itself, a skill worth learning for life during and after the joint. While you have so much time to reflect on the way you do business, give *special attention* to the section **Personal Ties** on page 28. When you stop and look at it, *everything* we do involves some kind of relationship. How well we can build and maintain ties between ourselves and the world has a very powerful impact on the quality of our lives.

HEALTH NEEDS IN THE JUNGLE

Not Arrested, SAVED!

> *"Man, you weren't arrested, you were saved! It was so cold up under those bridges they took pity on you and locked you up!"*

A lot of prisoners come off the streets in sad shape due to self-abuses of one form or another (booze, drugs, and general loose living). You can always knock off the speed freaks and crack heads because they look like they can slip between the bars. People who were burning themselves up often say that if it hadn't been for getting busted, they would have ended up on a slab. In short, their lives and health were out of control.

So let's face it, very few prisoners were health nuts on the streets. About the only exercise most outlaws get is running from the cops or stumbling out of topless joints at closing time! When you're strung out or ripping and running, you tend to treat your body like a chemical waste site. Plus, pulling a trigger is a far cry from an aerobic exercise!

As a result, you fall into prison in poor shape. Needless to say, a pen is not a health resort waiting to make you fit and firm. But you *have* to re-build with what's there or be trampled under foot. And let me stress that it IS possible to gain good health while locked up. As bad as it all may be, countless people all over the world have learned to survive and prosper on far less than you have in most U.S. prisons.

Survival of the Fittest

"A prison is a place where the vultures are always circling.
You don't want to be viewed as the next available carcass."

When it comes to taking care of themselves, there are basically two kinds of people. Those who do and those who don't. It's easy to tell the difference. The ones who don't are usually fat, slow, sloppy, sick a lot, depressed, stressed out, lazy, moody, withdrawn, vulnerable, and down on themselves. And keep in mind that people who don't treat themselves with respect don't earn respect from anyone else.

A joint is **definitely** not a place to be weak and unhealthy! This doesn't mean you must be a gorilla to survive, but you sure don't want to be viewed as a broken down "lame." Everyone knows who can take care of themselves and who cannot. It's reasonable to say that the weak and unhealthy are on the bottom of the prison pecking order. Therefore, every prisoner needs to be as healthy and together as possible. No matter what shape you're in now, it's time to make fitness a chief concern.

It's not easy to get healthy in prison. It demands constant effort and self-discipline. So what are the advantages of busting your ass to stay healthy? You get:

1) Strength of body: higher resistance to illness, more able to defend yourself, and better prepared to cope with adversity.

2) Stability of mind: a cooler attitude, more self-confidence, and lower stress and hostility levels.

3) Freedom to focus on spirit: improved mental focus, more peace of mind, and greater ability to concentrate and meditate.

4) Better preparation for release: much better control of short pains; not as quick to go off on anybody.

5) Increased success following release: far better prepared to cope with the free world on all levels, especially finding a job and developing positive personal relationships.

In order to be truly fit, you have to increase your overall health in a variety of areas: physical, mental, emotional, social, educational, spiritual, vocational, and cultural. This is the true way to do battle with the system, as we discussed in **Beating the System**. If you neglect any one of these areas, it will come back to haunt you because **that** is exactly where you'll be vulnerable! And the last thing you can afford in prison **or** in the community is an area of major weakness.

Stone Grocery Habit

"The old saying goes that a prisoner needs two things to survive: a cup of coffee and a cigarette."

Unfortunately, the emotional stress of prison often drives people to do unhealthy things just when they most need their health. If a prisoner or family member is depressed, angry, or lonely, they can get in the habit of eating, smoking, or using some other addictive behavior as a way of coping with their feelings. This happens a lot on the streets and can sneak up on you while you're down. What appears to be an escape or relaxation is really making your problems worse, whether you face that fact or not.

It's easy to tell ourselves that our situation is pure misery and so we deserve what little relief we can get. We're just looking for some excuse to let ourselves GO. This type of reasoning may have helped put us in prison. And our bodies and minds pay one hell of a price: short-term pleasure, long-term damage—not only to our health but to our self-respect and relationships with others.

We may get into chain smoking, coffee guzzling, or eating a lot of salty, greasy, sugary junk from the inmate store. This happens a lot to women prisoners when they miss their children or feel worthless or helpless. Some may have trouble dealing with the past, for instance if they have been sexually abused or thrown away by some dude they trusted. Or they may feel stupid for falling off into the same traps over and over. So they just let themselves go—eat to forget. Then they put on a lot of weight and end up feeling even worse! They pay the real price after release because none of their clothes fit and, most of all, they feel fat and ugly.

These problems can and must be avoided! In fact, exercise is one of the best stress relievers you can find. Spend your time in prison getting healthy, and you will walk out of this trip much better off.

A 10 Milky Way Day

"Morning and night I'd melt down 5 Milky Ways and drink 'um. What a sugar rush! The problem was the crash; it was like hitting a tank truck head on at 80!"

One of the first great shocks for everyone who goes down is having to face the stuff they drop on your tray and ask you to believe is food. If you didn't have to eat it to survive, you would think it was a joke off Saturday Night Live. Every place is different, some better than others, but none is the Holiday Inn. Overall it is shameful the cold-blooded things they do to totally defenseless food.

Equally important is the type of foods served: fats, starches, and sugar, with very little protein and complex carbohydrates. The items that do have good nutritional value are often cooked so poorly that people refuse to eat them. We used to use our pancakes as frisbees until one did serious brain damage to an assistant warden who stumbled into the line of fire!

What happens, of course, is that many people try to live out of the inmate store. Too bad if their mothers have to up the monthly social security check, just as long as poor Bobby doesn't have to look that cold oatmeal in the eye. Supporting a hungry prisoner can be a real hardship for loved ones on a limited budget. And living off the junk from the store causes some very serious health problems as well.

Granted, the zoozoos and whamwhams are more appealing than prison slop. But take a look at what's in them. Sugar, salt, fat, nicotine, caffeine, artificial flavors, preservatives, and a load of things you can't even pronounce! Not only is this stuff bad for you, many of these ingredients are stimulants that can make you edgy and out of control—a dangerous condition for a prisoner. The fact is, your diet has A LOT to do with your ability to control your feelings and actions.

One of the keys to health, in and out of prison, is the right diet. Although your choices are seriously limited in prison, you must learn to "eat smart." You have to choose the most useful and avoid the most harmful. Review the section **Physical Development** on page 24 for some ideas on how to improve your diet while in prison.

Staying Healthy in a Cage

> *"If you get seriously sick in a joint, you may as well make out a will and kiss your mother goodbye."*

The bad news is that *everyone* gets sick or hurt at some point while in prison. Some a little, some a lot. Many things come together to make prison a very unhealthy and dangerous place. Some dangers cannot be avoided. For instance, if one person in a cell block gets the flu from a visitor, everyone gets it. That's the main reason why so many leave prison with TB scars on their lungs.

Other dangers can sometimes be avoided. For example, some people get hurt while working on a tractor or in a metal shop, etc. Safety standards for prison labor are seldom carefully enforced. And everyone knows that it's easy to get off into a wreck with another inmate or the Man and end up needing a nose job. Since prison health care is not always up to free-world standards, it's smart to *stay alert*. Watch out for accidents or injuries which might require serious care or long-term treatment.

The good news is that *many* health problems can be avoided by simply taking care of yourself and using common sense. If you just follow the basic guidelines about food and exercise covered on page 24, you can stay reasonably healthy. The healthier your body and mind, the better your ability to avoid problems, fight off illness, and recover as quickly as possible. Always look for ways to stay warm and dry, get enough rest, eat right, exercise, etc. *Learn to take care of yourself.*

This doesn't mean that people who work on their health don't have problems, too. But they don't have as many or as often, nor as intense and long-lasting. Those who take care of themselves are *much more together*, far more alert, stronger, quicker, and a lot more confident.

By taking care, I don't mean being able to fight or simply giving your body what it wants when it wants it. I mean giving yourself the care and the respect required to keep you fit, alert, and best able to respond to the world around you. That often means saying "no" to what tastes or feels good because you respect your own well being. As an example, you have the good sense not to drink antifreeze. Why? Because although it is very sweet to the taste, it is poison. So too are many types of food, drink, and other substances which might give us immediate pleasure.

Some people walk into prison with health problems, such as diabetes, bad teeth, psychiatric problems, or a heart condition. This puts them in a bind, because if they demand help too loudly, they're labeled a "problem" and get shut down in one way or another. But if they are too humble and just go along for the ride, they won't get what they need.

When dealing with the medical personnel, be persistent but polite. Be patient but don't roll over and play dead; if you do, you are subject to end up that way. Try to be very "political"; ask a lot of questions from people who know what's happening and who's running things. Often inmate clerks control waiting lists, so a few cartons of smokes can work wonders. But beware of people who claim to be able to "fix things" and fail to come across. Like everything else, you have to learn who you can count on; so don't ever pay for *anything* in advance.

Just as important as physical health is the need to stay mentally strong. This is hard work in a joint, but a healthy, balanced mind is the foundation for everything you do. For many people depression is a constant enemy which eats away at their sense of hope. Depression is like a black hole which will absorb all of your energy if you let it. To combat it, you must never believe its lies that life is hopeless and meaningless. Keep pursuing your spiritual growth to find the strength and stability essential to survival. *Constantly* search for the fresh energy and insight you need to support your growth.

A Special Word about AIDS

The disease of the century is AIDS (autoimmune deficiency syndrome), and it is exploding in prisons across the country. There have been plenty of publicity and educational efforts to tell people how AIDS is spread and how to protect themselves. AIDS is a death sentence—one that people usually bring on themselves by having unprotected sex or sharing dirty needles. Outlaws are doing FAR more damage to themselves than the Man could ever hope to lay on them. Snap to the fact that it is not a man's disease, homosexual's disease, or white folks', black folks', or purple folks' disease. It kills *everyone* with total indifference!

So if you want to live, *protect yourself.* Make it a rule to use a condom during sex, and never share dirty needles. Learn more about staying healthy and avoiding AIDS. You can find sources of more information in **Additional Reading** on page 117.

If you know you have been exposed to AIDS or think you are at risk, get tested. Nobody wants to get that kind of bad news, but you'll feel better longer if you get some help now—both medical and emotional—to deal with the disease. And for God's sake, don't spread it! There is no glory in infecting a list of ignorant, careless fools who haven't got the sense to protect themselves.

DOING BATTLE WITH ANGER AND HATE

Anybody Seen My Armor?

> *"Like a turtle pulling into his shell for safety, a prisoner withdraws by trying to be less human, caring, feeling, and attached."*

From the day you pulled the chain, you've been gradually adapting to the loss of identity and respect, to the chaos and lurking danger, because you have to. In so doing, you've changed in a lot of subtle ways. Mostly you will go to any extreme not to be vulnerable to anyone or anything, at any time or under any circumstance! When you first rolled up, you may have stuck your neck out a few times because you weren't hip to what was happening—only to have someone try to bash your brains out. Logically, since you don't get off on pain, you quit.

By now you've learned that the prison trip consumes everything, so you must be on guard at all times. Day and night, seven days a week. To protect yourself you have slowly closed up on mental, spiritual, and physical levels. Now look within: have you become trapped in the very suit of armor you built to protect yourself?

If you notice you are losing the will or ability to make contact with people and things *outside of yourself,* your efforts for safety have become a trap. When you draw so far back that you become isolated from YOURSELF, you face the greatest danger of all, the loss of hope. If this occurs, the prisoner and family feel that nothing else exists but the distress of the moment. Remember: if hope dies, **everything** dies. Hope is a basic need…you must *never* give up!

I Hate Your Mama!

> *"The rage in my heart is like an atomic reactor that's gone into meltdown! God help the poor bastards who catch the fallout."*

Within the walls of concrete and steel, anger, pain, fear, and loneliness are the main courses on the menu. And, as you know, violence is often the dessert of choice. In addition, we are forced to accept often absurd rules and cope with insane pressures. When combined, these factors result in a dangerous charge of explosive **anger**. This anger spreads until we include everything and everyone in our blind **rage**.

We often use this rage in the way unlimited fuel dragsters use nitro: to propel us faster than the competition. Indeed, this may work for a few years, but it is extremely dangerous to us and to those around us. If we unleash it against the Man, other inmates, or ourselves, we face serious results. If we're not real careful, we can end up with fresh time or a tag on our big toe. And if we display it against our loved ones, as often happens in letters and visits, our most valued support can quickly vanish.

So we try to keep it all stuffed inside and handle the stress by doing more and more violence inside our heads. We may rehearse acts of vengeance and pretend to actually do them as a way to release the pressure. But as the rage continues to grow, it begins to force its way to the surface. It turns into hate and finally becomes our deep-seated **passion**. At this point, we may not be able to control ourselves any longer. We **must** find workable ways to deal with all this poison inside ourselves!

I can tell you from my personal experience that giving in to hate is like drinking battery acid. I know now that I carried guns in the streets *not* for protection but because I was looking for someone to give me an excuse to shoot them. And, sure enough, I found one. So for me, prison only amplified negative things which were already there, probably since childhood. Being in the joint simply made me *more* bitter and dangerous. But no matter where or when these feelings arise, each of us *can* and ***must*** learn to overcome our hostility. If we don't, we will be gradually swept away. Of the many dangers faced by a prisoner, NONE is more serious and far-reaching. Staying in control of this is tough, but I give you my word that its importance cannot be overstated.

A Walking Time Bomb

"I could hear the bomb ticking inside my head. It kept getting louder and louder until I wanted to scream!"

Living behind a tidal wave of anger is a way of trying to protect ourselves from pain and fear. It is as though anger and violence become a drug we use to release stress or cover up our pain for a short time. We gradually buy in to the false idea that whoever is close to us must be the cause of our pain and that our needs can be met by going off on people. In the end, we convince ourselves that the ideal way to solve our problems is to "go nuclear."

In this frame of mind, you can give yourself "permission" to actually do the mad-dog, radical things you used to only think about. It may happen in the joint or after release, when you least expect it. Again, this is a *very serious danger*. Not only do you run the risk of killing or being killed, you become a prime target for the prison staff, other inmates, state police, etc. All this does is to take a bad situation and make it worse.

Take a good look in the mirror. Look back behind your eyes: do you see an explosive charge, *always* looking for something to set you off? If so, you need to learn to control it now. Or after three or four years in a joint you will blindly hate *everything and everybody.* This includes the system, those around you, and, too often, yourself and those who love you. When you're overflowing with rage, you talk war and often take out your stress on those around you, even when you don't mean to. If this happens you have sentenced **yourself** to permanent exile, crushing any hope of rewarding bonds with family, friends, employers, and folks you've yet to meet. This is just another trap to steal a deeper part of your mind and soul!

So, if you find yourself wishing you were the Terminator and could snuff everybody, *you have a problem!* This is a danger sign that cannot be ignored. Find the courage and help to overcome your demons or they will eat you from the inside out. To do this, you **must** learn to control and direct your mind so that no one and nothing can make you dance like a puppet on a string.

Whenever you feel your anger about to erupt, it is **essential** that you confront and deal with it. You must recognize and work through your feelings. **Be very careful:** teach yourself to call a time out before you go off on somebody. WATCH how you are dealing with what's happening both inside and outside of you. Observe the way your mind is working. Step back, settle down, and see it all happening! LISTEN to how your mind talks to itself, to its tone and content.

Stay alert! Are you reacting to *real problems* or something of your own making? Is your reaction going to make things better or worse? What do you really want to get out of this situation? What choices do you have? Your ability to control how your mind and emotions respond is the *one true freedom* you have! While you cannot control the daily events of your life, you *can* and *must* control the ways you think and act! Don't react out of blind instinct; think about what's happening and respond in a way that is appropriate and useful. Review **Reshape Your Thinking** on page 17 for more ideas on ways to take control of your thoughts and actions.

Catch a Grip!

> *"These people think I'm bad? Hell, I'll show them what 'bad' really is!!"*

At first it made you sick to watch the truly insane stuff that goes down in prison, but after awhile you got numbed out in order to cope. As you watched the vile corruption around you, you began to develop a burning bitterness toward the system and the world that created it. For many inmates this means taking on a hostile attitude, an outlaw mentality, to help them survive and handle the pain. After years of bitterness and isolation, people sometimes take a strange pride in being an outcast, a "stone outlaw." For those who have been stripped of power and self-esteem, this can be a way to find an identity for themselves, even if a negative one.

Plus, prisoners sit around and tell endless lies and war stories about their gangster days and plans for future capers. Most of this is just a way to kill time, but it also feeds the feeling of "me against the square world." As time passes it's not surprising if you become consumed with the role of a professional outlaw. It provides a strong motivator, a fire that keeps your spirit alive! But be aware of the ultimate price: you can become a slave to something even more demanding than the Man. The farther you fall off into this pit, the farther you have to climb out again! There is nothing to be gained by becoming an "Ex-con from Hell." I learned this lesson the hard way.

Just because you watch others lose their grip doesn't mean you have to! Taking on a "ballistic" attitude and telling yourself you're a dangerous character may keep your motor running when you feel like you're out of gas. But it quickly becomes a personal demon. Don't buy in to the scam that you have to be a raging bad ass in order to keep your pride and dignity alive. This attitude is totally self-destructive; people who believe it will be a prisoner of themselves *long* after their bodies are released. You **must not** let this happen!! Being a captive of the State is bad enough; becoming a captive of self-provoked madness is totally uncool.

Your biggest problems will come *after* release as you strive to shed the prison mind set and build a useful life. Prison games don't work in the community because the **rules** are different! Although both worlds can be heavy and strange, each calls for different ways of viewing life and responding to it. Keep in mind that the more you play the prison game, the more garbage you have to carry out with you. The ONLY thing prison values will do for you in the free world is put you right back in the pen. Doing time and hitting the bricks are hard enough; don't make them impossible by setting yourself up to fail!

It will be easier to handle your feelings if you keep physically healthy and fit. Study **Physical Development** (page 24) and **Health Needs in the Jungle** (page 52) for suggestions on how to keep your body in shape. Healthy foods and exercise can make it easier to keep your emotions calm and under control. And if you can find a friend, minister, or professional counselor to talk to, it will help you let off steam and get a different viewpoint on what is happening and other ways you can respond.

But the only long-term way to overcome hate and anger is through *growth*. It's only when you are focused on your own self-improvement that the garbage around you loses its importance. And it's only when you can look at yourself with pride and see how far you've come that you can forget about what others have done and what you'd like to do to them. There's only one real answer: outgrow the anger. Replace it with pride and peace of mind! So go back, review **Beating the System** (page 7), and put it into practice. **DO IT NOW!** If you let anger take over, then the system has won and you are a permanent part of the maze.

In the joint or in the streets, you must keep your mind and heart strong, honest, and focused in order to adjust to change without being eaten alive!! Life in prison is, after all, just a lesson in how to come to grips with adversity. This challenge is always with us, no matter where we are.

Believe it or not, this issue is equally important for family and friends of prisoners. Unless they find positive, healthy ways to balance their pain, loneliness, and fear, their lives get swallowed up in depression and anger. Study the section **Advice for Families** on page 93 for ways to understand and deal with all this.

COPING WITH HARD TIME

Everything's Bad—That's Good!

"Some stand up and grow strong, some wither and die. It's the same game but different players play it different ways."

So here you are, locked down like a rabid dog, being treated like you're ugly and stupid. No one in their right mind would seek such a plight. What you face as a convict is one of the most painful challenges anyone can experience.

But your situation has some hidden benefits that you may not recognize. Suffering is an essential part of everyone's life. From birth to death, we endure an inescapable series of painful events. As crazy as it may seem, pain can point the way toward growth. The more we suffer, the deeper we can look into our spiritual nature. And the more our spiritual nature deepens, the better we can understand reality and the secrets of life.

Thus, the pain we endure as prisoners can force us to grow farther than we ever would have in the free world. But this will only happen if we stand up, face our suffering, and do battle with it! Many of us try to escape the pains of life by taking shelter in drugs, gambling, sexual extremes, or getting lost in another person. This won't solve our problems, but it *will* distract us from any possibility of learning from our suffering!

We also cannot gain from our labors if we *surrender* to the madness or sorrow of the moment. The loss of hope, just giving up, is an age-old trap! We need faith and determination to break out of blind despair. With every step forward, we gain a greater store of personal strength and insight. So, in a strange way, facing our suffering brings us rewards that cannot be gained any other way. This is why suicide (of mind, body, or spirit) is such a waste: when we give up, we lose the chance to use our stress and pain to promote our growth.

NOW is the time to commit yourself to use the pressure and hardship of the moment to temper your will, strengthen your mind, discipline your body, improve your judgment, and prepare for the future, be it a week away or 20 years. Use your suffering to awaken you to greater depths of feeling and insight. If you have to go through this garbage, why not get as much out of it as possible?

Nice idea, but it's a hell of a lot easier said than done! First, think of your situation as *survival training*. There isn't any school in the world that will teach you what you can learn about yourself and others inside a joint! This is not to say you want to be there, but while you are, **why not use it to the max?** Watch how you think and act; examine your values and behavior on *every* level.

Don't just lie on your bunk and listen to your heart beat. Have the honesty and courage to face what you find inside yourself. Anything you don't like or that doesn't work *can be changed!* While folks are running around in the streets eaten up with nickel and dime garbage, you have a rare chance to search for the roots of who you are and what you want your life to be. Make prison work for you. Take your punishment and turn it into triumph!

Say, Did My Watch Stop?

*"My cell partner said time had stopped. I looked at my watch
and told him he was crazy; it was running backwards."*

Doing time, in prison or on the streets, works in cycles. There are high and low points. At the low times everything seems to **STOP**. This usually happens after a crisis, such as when an appeal or parole falls through. A family crisis, such as an unexpected divorce or the death of a loved one, can also make the clock seem to quit ticking.

These are dangerous periods; hope gets thin and both inmates and loved ones think, "Why bother?" Be careful when things go into a depressed state. It's easy to slide off into a "don't give a damn" attitude. If you become consumed with sad and desperate feelings, it usually leads to crazy or violent behavior, and this only compounds the problems. But don't lose faith: as long as the sun keeps coming up and going down, time IS passing.

The secret to dealing with these slow times is to **keep busy**! Beware of stress, depression, and self-pity. Don't just sit around and pick your nose; and becoming a TV junkie won't fix things, either. Find ways to challenge your mind and develop your body. This is not a time to just glide along! Get involved in something positive, and everything will work out. Remember: while there are many physical limits on you, what you can do inside your head is *boundless!*

For Long Termers and Lifers

*"For most people prison is just a chapter in their lives, but
for some it's the whole damned book!"*

For the past 15 years, state legislatures and the U.S. Congress have passed more laws putting more people away for longer periods. All it takes is for one mad dog ex-con to do something really gross. Citizens are outraged and scream for the blood of "all those criminals." So ambitious politicians sponsor new laws to show they are champions in the "war against crime." As a result, they pass no-mercy sentencing guidelines, harsher habitual criminal statutes, elimination of parole, and tons of other items off the D.A.'s wish list as a way to "flush" you rather than "punish" you.

So how does all this advice serve those who are ***trapped*** in the maze? What use is it to men and women who have been "thrown away" and have no choice but to adjust and cope? I'm not talking here about the "turn arounds" who get out before they know how to find the chow hall. I mean those of you who are being ground up and fed to the hogs! For lifers and people doing **serious** time, many things in this book may appear useless. They may not seem to relate to someone doing more time than King Kong could carry.

All this rah-rah jive about personal growth—does it *really* make any sense for a five-time loser looking at 2022 for relief? It may not seem to on the surface. You have to stop and *really* look at it. One can say, "I'm a lifer, so why bother to care, to try, or even hope?" But that is an emotional reaction based on a moment of depression, a sad point of view. The truth is: *life is not over till it's over!* So the *more* time you have to carry, the *more* you need strength of mind and heart, and the more the ideas in this book apply to **YOU**. Frankly, the need for personal development is 100 times greater for someone doing 10 years than a person doing 10 months!

We were not born to "party hardy" but to come to an ever growing understanding of ourselves. Every moment we live is a new and unique chance to find greater inner power and peace. No matter how harsh, *anything* that forces us to look life in the eye gives us a chance to *be more!* With this point of view, we can work toward the true goal of life just as effectively in prison as anywhere else.

It is of little comfort to a prisoner doing serious time, but in truth you are very different from 99% of mankind. While the public is caught up in the countless distractions of daily life, you don't have to wade through the silly trash that eats people up in the streets. Even though you didn't choose it, your situation frees you to go within yourself and explore remote and secret corners of your mind and spirit.

This chance to get away from the folly of the world is the condition that monks and wise men have sought for centuries. For a person who has so much time they cannot see light at the end of the tunnel, you can achieve your freedom by looking within yourself and letting go of old cravings and attachments. Granted, a joint is not a monastery filled with peaceful vibes! But after five years or more, life in prison just becomes the same old routine. So you can shift your attention and use the time as a unique chance to **focus within**! Use it, treasure it, take advantage of this chance to find truth within the center of your being. There is a world within you just as great and powerful as the world outside of you. Find it, explore it, learn to live in that deeper reality!

Never Surrender Your Mind!

> *"Prisoners have two things they truly own: the power of their wills and the quality of their minds."*

By now you've been down more than a few Christmas Eves—so you are no stranger to the insanity of a cell block! You know that, when a person is being held by force and threatened with severe punishment, it is often necessary for them to comply with the defined rules of daily life. But being a captive does *not* mean you should abandon yourself! It is not necessary for you to sink into the quicksand of dishonesty, hatred, isolation, bitterness, and *hopelessness* that spread in prison like a fungus. Just because a prison has your body, it cannot command your will or your mind—unless you surrender them. No matter who does what to mess with you, you must **never**, **ever** surrender control of your dignity, hope, or mental processes. It doesn't matter if you are doing 20 months or 20 flat years, the principle is the same.

If your body is attacked and you don't die, it *can* heal. If you get lost in depression but refuse to give up, you *can* recover. And when someone jacks with your understanding, you can fight their influence and get your balance back. Your ability to think and reason is your tie to reality, and it's 100% *yours*. It gives you the capacity to grow and the will to hold on against all obstacles. Cherish and protect it at all costs!!

The best way to hold on to yourself while surviving captivity is to build a safe haven within yourself. *Not* just a brief escape from your pain but a positive, constructive way to weather *all* the storms that threaten to overwhelm you. Even though the world around you is sick and shallow, that doesn't mean you must be the same. Fight back by finding and following your own sense of values. **Personal growth** is the only life raft you have when you get this far out to sea! Although your progress may seem slow, your will power and self-respect grow stronger every time you refuse to let the energy of the joint "take" you.

Reflect, meditate, go within to develop your spiritual nature. Read, study, help others, learn to draw, write science fiction, play baseball, make belts, feed the birds in the yard, write poetry, stay in touch with world events, work out, play music. Do *anything* positive or healthy to keep from getting lost in prison dishonor, self-pity, and anger against yourself and/or the world. Although things around you are ugly and stupid, you can find beauty and a reason for hope within your own heart and will. But it will not just come to you. As when searching for a precious diamond, you must dig deep to find it.

LOOKING FOR THE DOOR

The Carrots: Appeals, Pardons, and Paroles

"Nose first or toes first, everyone gets out!"

Clearly the first two rules concerning prison life are **to survive** and **to get out**! And most inmates do, in fact, live through it and finally exit. There are different ways people try to obtain release. The "creative" ways are hitting the fence, digging a tunnel, dressing up like a nun, etc. The traditional—and more permanent—ways are appeals, pardons, and paroles. Most people end up being released on parole.

As we discussed on page 42, an inmate and family often hold themselves together after sentencing by hoping for a successful appeal. After a few years of intense effort and concern, that doesn't work so they may decide to push for a pardon. A pardon, in most cases, is just grasping at straws; the odds against it are so great *no inmate should expect it to be successful.*

Successful pardons (or time cuts or commutations of sentence) are as rare as hen's teeth. In some cases, they are based on the merits of the case or the reversal of an unjust sentence. But more often, the very few pardons granted are political favors, and most inmates and families just don't have the juice (power and money) to make that happen. You *may* have a shot if the real villain finally confesses, the D.A. requests a commutation, and the media backs it. And you know how rare such things are.

My experience suggests that most people try for appeals and/or pardons for two reasons. Their sentence is so heavy they cannot see daylight and this is the way they choose to keep from giving up. Or they are looking for a way to occupy themselves as they build enough time to become eligible for parole.

If you want to go after an appeal or a pardon, the best general rule is to *do your homework first*. Don't put your fate in the hands of a jail house lawyer if you can help it. Although some are very competent, you are often wasting your hope and groceries. You should certainly learn all you can from inmates who have insight and experience. But appellate law is THE most complex aspect of criminal law and requires some very special skills which few prisoners have. Study the laws and get all the help you can inside. Then, if you think you have a shot and are within the time limits, try to get your case (and transcripts) before an appeals attorney on the streets.

Warning: do not invest your life savings in an appeal, pardon, or parole effort! It's not necessary and in most cases will not do any good. Also, beware lawyers or private consultants who take advantage of an inmate's or family's desperation by giving them false hopes. If you hire an attorney, have a well-defined contract *and* a clear idea of how long it will take. Many such efforts take YEARS and the prisoner is already free by the time the appeals court rules!

So for most people, release comes by parole or discharge at a defined date. If you have a probable release date, then for better or worse, you *know* what you're looking at. But if you are dealing with a state parole process, it can be a big guessing game. Parole can become the Great Crusade for both the inmate and loved ones. Often everyone looks forward to it and makes a huge *investment* of time, energy, money, and, most of all, hope. It can be a long, draining ordeal and drag you into a state of deep emotional distress. The danger comes when you place *all* your hopes and resources on any one effort for release. If the bottom falls out, you don't have anything else to stand on!

The Old Turn Down Blues

*"Say, didn't you hear me? I **said** I was sorry!"*

Keep in mind that the appeals, pardons, and parole processes are *just* as insane and hard to understand as the court and the prison system. In addition, the institution often has control over your good time rates and awards, which really keeps you dancing. So don't be shocked if they jack you around, string you out, give you false hopes, and *then* cut your throat.

Try to be prepared for the mental and emotional let down that comes with a turn down, denial, or set off. There are no words to describe it but anyone who has lived it will fully understand. This event is *equally* hard on the family because they have often placed all their hopes for relief on the success of this effort. The natural reaction is disappointment and wanting to know why. Don't be surprised if you never get a straight answer. Punishment is far from an exact science.

Remember that the final goal is to get out **and stay out**, so save some mental and physical resources for the future. If you invest everything in each new effort, three or four denials or set-offs can throw a prisoner and his family into mental, emotional, and even financial bankruptcy. This is another blind turn in the maze and can lead to expanded bitterness and burn out. No matter where you are in the process, don't let the system or your false hopes break you or your loved ones.

My advice to **both** inmates and families: no matter how crazy or heavy things get, don't crawl off under a log and die. It's OK to pause and rest from time to time but you **must** do whatever it takes to keep yourself strong and united. The appeal, pardon, and parole processes are but single steps in this whole journey; don't let them eat you. Whatever happens, *stay cool* and don't go off on anybody. Hope for the best but be prepared for the worst. Some folks get out sooner, some later. Your time will come, so hang on. If you lose hope now, they have you forever!

GETTING SHORT

99 Days & A Get Up

> *"I held my breath the last 90 days and pretended I was the Invisible Man!"*

It's odd how different people count their time. A person doing a dime counts years. A person doing a year counts months. A person doing months counts days. And a person doing days counts hours. Each has a different frame of mind but all have a common goal: freedom! So for each, release becomes the top priority, often excluding all other factors.

When an inmate finally begins to get short, he or she goes through a whole bunch of conflicting, frightening thoughts and feelings. For someone who has only been down 12 months in a work camp, it will be much more light-weight than for someone who has been buried for 12 years in Leavenworth. The more times the world has turned since an inmate fell off into prison, the more dizzy he or she will be the day they are kicked out.

When you get down to 100 days or so from exit everything gets real weird. Most inmates and families feel an intense mixture of hope and fear about what the future holds. You get nervous and edgy and it looks like the Man is trying to trap or goad you into making a bad move. And on top of every problem, you have to cope with the hardest factor to control, **yourself.**

These "short pains" are **very** real and affect both the mind and body. This is a time of extreme anxiety when everyone tries to gear up and get ready. You may get the strong impression that those around you are out to get you. And, look here, they probably are! As you know, jealously is a monster inside the small world of a prison. So be super careful to avoid any heat from any source. And, whatever you do, don't run around telling everyone, "Man, I'm so short I could fit my whole body into a match box!" Just keep your mouth shut!

As you struggle to prepare for release, inmates **and** their loved ones should get a copy of *99 Days & A Get Up* (see inside back cover). This small book can help take the edge off a scary time and prepare you for life after prison. Use this material to help you prepare your survival plan and to get your head ready for the shift. Also study *Man, I Need a Job!* (inside back cover) to prepare for getting and keeping a job. Job hunting is a real challenge and you owe it to yourself to be as ready as possible. And if you have **any** form of dependency or addiction problem, read *Life Without a Crutch* (inside back cover) as an important step in staying free and enjoying life.

The Moment of Truth

"On the surface you try to look mellow. You don't want anybody to know that inside your guts it's like Custer's last stand!

Now, as you strive to get ready to hit the bricks, you feel as though you are about to play a game of world-class poker with a pair of deuces! All the anxiety you went through when you first went down comes roaring back. With it come sleepless nights, loss of appetite, and six tons of stress and dread.

As you get *really short*, fear of the unknown begins to nibble at your brain like a hungry rat. The same concerns affect your family and loved ones. They get really worried that suddenly Mr. Bad Ass or Ms. Trouble is actually coming home. What will happen? More of the same?? Were the promises real?!? This is a moment of truth. If you have spent years feeding yourself and the world a lot of jive or living off false hopes, **NOW** is the time to get your heart and head right.

Your mind plays a LOT of tricks on you the closer you get to the door. You just *know* in your heart something horrible is going to happen to prevent your actual exit. A new detainer? A screw up in the paper work!? A set up and five years new time!?! It gets *real crazy!* The last week is sheer agony. No sleep, not much food...just holding your breath. Trying hard not to give off any "I'm short" vibes. Staying away from old enemies; dodging the hacks who hate you. Wanting to give your stuff away to the few you care about but being too paranoid to do it.

NOW is a good time to do a mental and emotional inventory, sorting out the positive lessons you've learned from the junk you've collected. Make every effort to recognize and eliminate the mental and emotional garbage that's built up in prison. As we've seen, such feelings often become a way of life. If so, you may not even realize how angry or hostile you have become. But unless you're St. Peter, you probably have *many* negative emotions going on deep inside.

A week before I left the joint the second time, I wrote a list of the things that had most hurt and angered me. In my mind I thought it would only take 30 minutes and one page of paper. In fact it took three days and nights and a full notebook! It was shocking to uncover the mountain of bad feelings I had against so many things and people, especially myself (not to mention the snitch). Then, the night before I left, I put the notebook in a trash can, soaked it with lighter fluid, lit the sucker up—and laughed a LOT! It is *so* important to do everything you can to leave your anger and "attitude" behind. In your mind, declare your roles as "slave" and as "criminal" to be **over**: let them go! Do NOT walk out the gate with this old baggage.

It is vital to relax, do a lot of deep breathing, and practice extra patience on all fronts. Surely the last thing you want to do is get sideways with *anyone*. The safest approach is to get real quiet, stick to yourself, and begin to cut yourself loose from the way things are done in the pen. (But be careful not to let your mind leave while your body is still inside.)

This is also the time to look at the very powerful issue of FEAR. It does no good to pretend it doesn't exist. The longer you've been down, the greater your discomfort will be over the uncertain future. You will naturally feel stress about your upcoming role in the free world. But the work you've done inside yourself while a captive and the quality of your plans will help keep the stress under control. Chill out, focus on self-control, and don't sweat the small stuff.

It's not unusual to feel guilty or sad for getting to leave while people you care about are still stuck shuffling up and down the halls. But you didn't carry them in with you and you don't get to carry them out. Everyone has their yoke to pull; their turn will come, too. Just give them all your gear, wish 'um well, and move on.

REBIRTH AND BEYOND: RELEASE TO SUCCESS

THE RUSH OF RELEASE

Kicked Out of the Joint!

"When they came to cut me loose I told 'um I had some unfinished business, to come back in an hour. The Major said leave NOW or be drug out feet first. They never were big on hospitality!"

The day they cut you loose begins like any other: the sun comes up, the shifts change, and the joint slips into its dull old routine. One would think that after all your excitement and expectation there should be a parade with marching bands and a cheering crowd. But, no, they just tell you to pack your shit, sign some papers, and get the hell off government property. Ready or not, **you get kicked out!**

As you ride away and look back, all you see are faceless people doing what you did yesterday and countless mornings before that. The only difference is that tonight someone else will be in your bunk—because **you're damn well gone!**

Suddenly you perceive that this place, which has been the center of your life for so long, is nothing more than a tiny fly speck on the side of a narrow little backroad, outside of a quiet little town. The *only* thing that ever gave it any importance was your presence. Then you turn away and face forward—into the future with all its challenges, options, risks, and rewards.

Your space ship has now returned from Penal Colony X to Planet Earth and beamed you down to an noisy, nasty Greyhound bus station. The return is as shocking as the day you pulled the chain! Remember what you went through adjusting to the joint? Now you begin to go through the same thing, except *backwards*, as you start the long process of adjusting to the streets. The deeper they had you buried and the longer you've been away, the harder it will be, because so much has changed. Indeed, ***everything*** has changed—especially ***you.***

Wow, I'm OUT—or Am I??!

"So tell me the truth, is my brand showing?"

The day you hit the bricks, you will not feel "free." In fact, aside from your desire to get the hell down the road, you may not feel much of anything, because you will be numb. This is perfectly natural. Your body and mind are working overtime to absorb all the changes that come with suddenly being thrown into the insanity and speed of modern life. If you're like most folks, you just go into a mild state of shock. It would be no different if suddenly you returned from five years on an island in the South Pacific. Your body is *out here*, but the rest of you is still *back there*.

Don't let this worry you. There is nothing you can do to change or hurry things up. Just understand what's going on and try to relax and flow with it. Keep telling yourself to calm down and accept the fresh wonder of it all. Try to suspend your mind and simply experience the explosion of new sights and sounds. The first week or two are sort of a blur. In fact, many newly released people say they feel as though they are on a furlough and not really free.

As the initial shock begins to wear off, the first thing you feel is *different* from everyone else. It is as if squares can look at you and see "CRIMINAL" branded across your forehead. This is a strong feeling that cannot just be ignored, but it's absolute rubbish. The only time your past really shows is if you play gangster, let your anger hang out, or run the dull old game of "scare the squares."

The second thing you experience is *depression!* This is very confusing because you expect someone just out of prison to be on top of the world. But the extreme nature of the changes you must make is very unsettling and draining. Relax: you are not going crazy. Such feelings are a natural part of the radical shift in reality an ex-con faces. They may come and go over the first year or so before you have your balance. In most cases, they will simply pass with time. However, if you find yourself being overwhelmed by depression, or any emotion, **go get help**!

One thing for sure: release from captivity IS an exciting and wonderful event. To suddenly move from a state of no choice into one of abundant options can be the rush of a lifetime. Like blasting full speed down the steep bank of a roller coaster, it's a sensational **thrill**! Savor the moment!!

Be Cool, Fool

> *"A former prisoner can be a living hand grenade, just walking around looking mellow until some small thing pulls his or her pin."*

While in prison, many people lose touch with their feelings and can't recognize what's actually buried inside. When this happens, they may feel calm and in control for a few weeks or months after release, only to go into fits of irrational behavior, anger, or depression later on. This is often brought to the surface by anxiety from two classic traps: *wanting too much too soon* and *expecting the impossible*.

The anxiety doesn't really hit you at first because you're busy just looking around and enjoying the show. But as you accept your freedom and try to start functioning, the stress of so many changes can bring up old feelings. If you don't deal with these buried feelings, they may explode. You will find yourself reacting to a new situation with old prison ways of thinking and acting. You'll hear it coming out of your mouth! Although this is a natural result of having been in prison, it can seriously endanger your welfare and ties throughout the community.

Prison may not be to blame for all of these feelings. For many folks, their attitude put them in the joint to begin with. That attitude may have come from past abuse—physical and emotional scars they received as a child. As adults, they may not understand where those scars came from or what to do about them. And prisons have a 200-year history of making the damage much worse!

But no matter how much abuse we've suffered (both in and out of prison), it doesn't justify passing our pain on to others. Too often we act out against the very people who stood by us, or total strangers who just happen to be on hand. We must beware of this trap. It will crush our hope for the future and kill any chance of getting along with others, not to mention getting us locked up again.

On top of everything else, you will **know** that what you're doing is not right for your new situation. But you don't have the skills yet for a more practical response. When you are fresh out, you still have a foot in both worlds. This leads to a LOT of confusion and mental torment, so slow down and give yourself some slack. ***Cool your jets!***

If you find yourself doing any of the above, take it seriously. Don't just try to look the other way! Many ex-cons ignore disruptive thoughts or actions until things get out of control and they are in a major crisis. They may try to cope by getting stoned just to "take the edge off," but this does nothing to resolve their problems. A few hours later the problems are still right there, even worse than before!

So keep an eye on your pressure gauge. When you see the needle approaching the red zone, go find a friend, minister, or counselor to help you cope with this difficult time. Many people don't bother to seek help because the joint has fooled them into thinking they are totally alone and cut off from the world. Many prisoners get into the ego trip of thinking that a *real man* shouldn't need help from others or that no one could possibly understand them. But this attitude is false. In truth, there **ARE** capable people who understand what you are going through and can help you develop the skills to work through your feelings. So don't hesitate to seek and accept *any* type of help that will improve the quality of your life.

Now What?!?

> *"Sleeping under a piano crate, standing in a soup line, and living like a bum is NOT my idea of freedom!"*

Every person who exits a jail or prison must deal with basic survival needs. In order to meet these needs, a realistic plan is essential. (Planning for the future is discussed in more depth in ***99 Days & A Get Up*** and ***Man, I Need a Job!***— see inside back cover). Most prisoners try to construct a plan while down, but after release they quickly find that it was based more on **hope** than **fact**. When this happens, they must be ready to revise their plans, daily if needed.

When we are in a survival mode, we tend to let everything slide except our immediate needs. We think about only what is in front of us. This is normal and necessary. It was also the primary way of life in prison. But in order to build a balanced life, we need to work from a balanced plan that takes all of our needs into consideration. As we make progress, we can shift some of our attention, energy, and resources from survival to other parts of our plan.

To be balanced, a basic survival plan should include:

1. A survival budget and source of needed funds
2. Employment
3. Family/personal support (including child care, if needed)
4. Housing
5. Transportation
6. Health care
7. Legal concerns and parole
8. Recreation
9. Personal growth: education and training
10. Spiritual nourishment and growth

Some of these areas focus on basic get-down survival, while others are part of our long-term development, as discussed in **Balance Your Growth** on page 21. Plans are best developed in two time frames: short-term (the first six to 12 months) and long-term (the next two to five years). As short-term needs are met, our emphasis will shift to long-term growth and self-improvement. To help reduce some of the confusion and anxiety, it is also smart to create a specific plan just for that first, crazy week on the streets.

There is limited support available in the community to help you meet some of your survival needs. But the help won't come looking for you. Nobody in the free world thinks they owe you a favor because you've done a taste of time. And the rumors about wonderful programs such as Supplemental Security Income (SSI) and Small Business Administration (SBA) loans just waiting for released prisoners are total garbage. Ninety-nine percent of your progress will depend on you to make realistic plans and then to find and use the opportunities you need. The handbook *Man, I Need a Job!* (see inside back cover) gives more information on finding help in the community.

A special word of caution: over the past 26 years I have watched countless ex-cons struggle with the difference between what they want and what they can get. Next to anger and isolation, no other single thing seems to create so much stress. There is an intense drive to get back up as quickly as possible, but it **never** happens fast enough or to the degree hoped for. Again, do not set yourself up to fail by expecting too much from yourself and the world.

It helps to think of yourself as *new to town*, which is true. And with any newcomer, certain dues are required. For someone moving from Dallas to Seattle, it may take three years to get settled and five years to get even half way comfortable. The best way to cope is to set small goals that can be achieved in the near future. Rather than plan to "get a good job paying $40,000 a year," plan to "get up tomorrow at 7 a.m. and go fill out applications at the four places you called today." Your progress for the first few years will be painfully slow. But keep yourself under control and you will watch your progress grow like a snowball rolling down a hill!

Man, I Need a Job!

> *"A job is important not only for survival but because it offers a valuable way to begin feeling better about yourself after the joint."*

Shortly after release a former prisoner has to deal with the need for a job. A job is a basic part of survival and meeting the rules of parole. For ex-cons, this presents a series of special problems based on the economy, a criminal record, fear of failure, lack of current skills, the need for transportation, and many others.

Finding and keeping a job is hard even for well-prepared squares. It is far more difficult for people with a criminal past! So it makes sense to do as much preparation as you can toward success in the job market. A lot of what it takes to get and keep a job is **mental**. Although you may not actually score a gig from inside a cell, you can be setting goals, learning new skills, and working on your attitude and self-control. Your mental attitude determines your self-confidence and the way you present yourself. Therefore, the better you come to terms with your own criminal history, the better you'll be able to look an employer in the eye and sell your value as a person.

Before *and* after release, you can help yourself prepare to find a job by reading *Man, I Need a Job!* (see inside back cover). This handbook discusses general job search skills as well as ways to deal with your criminal history. You should continue to review it during your actual job search, while adjusting to the work place, and later when you're ready to look for a better job. There are some unique attitudes and skills an ex-con really *needs* to prepare for a rewarding job. A lot of useful ideas will jump out at you just when you need them.

THE FIRST TASTE OF FREEDOM

A New World, A New You

> *"It's an all-new game. New rules, new players and the score is 0 to 0. Use what you learned in the joint but if you pistol whip your mother, you're going to catch a penalty."*

Getting out is one side of the coin; staying out is the other. Release from prison is NOT the solution to your problems! It's just the *midpoint* of a much larger, more complex experience. In a sense, it's as if you are being reborn. The ways of thinking and acting you picked up in prison are now **dead and stinking**! Along with all the anxiety and confusion of release, you have the chance to decide who you really want to be.

Inmates carry tons of garbage out of prison with them. They often hit the streets consumed with hostile feelings and less in control of themselves than the day they went down. Plus, they tend to show mistrust and blind resentment toward everything and everybody they come into contact with. So it's normal for people just out to feel anxious and lost at times.

Many ex-cons try to handle their uncertainty with hostility and jail house jive. But this just keeps you isolated from those around you. If you *want* to be rejected and fail to get along with anyone, all you have to do is play Professional Ex-Con. I admit that I wore my mean mask for a long time because I thought it would protect me from the vultures. Perhaps it did in a few cases. But it also cut me off from any hope of loving or being loved. I mean, who wants to kiss a cobra? Only another cobra! And that's not the kind of company you want to keep.

Until you are able to become a part of the world after release, you're not yet free. The Man still has you! Although it only took one heart beat for your body to leave the joint, your mind won't leave until it has something more positive to attach itself to! So kick back and be patient. As time passes you will focus more on street issues and less on prison war games. It just takes a little effort and a lot of patience. You can do it.

In addition to hostility and mistrust, being locked up can also cause prisoners to lose their sense of *identity and purpose.* Thus it's normal for a person fresh out to wonder who they are or how they should carry themselves. The basic rule in society is this: you are what you do! As discussed in **Seek the Right Path** (page 15), if you act in positive ways which result in benefits for yourself *and* the world around you, you're a "good" person, worthy of respect and support. On the other hand, if you act in negative, selfish ways that benefit you at the expense of others, you're a "bad" person. You can expect to be disliked, rejected, and possibly punished.

Life in the joint says you have to be nasty and cold-blooded to get over on others. The question is, do you want to be a slave to an idea that results in failure and rejection? Or are you ready to find a new way to relate to yourself and other people? One key to true freedom and satisfaction is having the respect of *both* yourself and others. To score this, you have to be right with people, giving them the respect, kindness, honesty, tenderness, and concern that you yourself hunger for.

As you re-establish contact with family and friends, try to lighten up; relax and take it easy. With new people, be cautious and take your time, but also stay open to an exchange of energy and concern. This doesn't mean it's always safe to be a trusting, decent person. From time to time some shark will come along and try to pick your bones clean. Clearly there IS risk attached to being an honest, caring human being. But if you use the insight you've learned in the joint and the streets, you will be *very careful* who you let get next to you. Pick your shot. It's smart business to be selective—but don't run and hide!

Becoming a good person doesn't require being a chump. It means basing your thoughts and actions on what you believe is decent and right. Stay alert. Don't be guided by what looks good, smells sweet, or tells you what you want to hear. *That's* probably what put you in the joint to begin with. I'm sure you understand.

Relighting the Flame

"The first year I was down, fun died. The second year, laughter; the third, tenderness; the fourth, love. By the time they finally cut me loose, there was nothing left but echoes."

One of the hardest and most important adjustments ex-cons have to make is in dealing with people. Life on the streets and in prison breeds mistrust of strangers. At the same time, it tends to distance you from your ability to be **intimate and loving**. You can "think it," write poems about it, dream of it, but you don't really know how to do it!

Hear me: the walls you build to protect yourself from others can become your own prison. They end up keeping you in and everybody else out, even the ones you want to let in. In this way your heart becomes a lonely castle with a draw bridge you've forgotten how to let down. Your mind remembers how it used to be, but all the gears and chains are so rusty nothing works the way it should. This is a real problem when you come back to someone you love and with whom you want to be deeply personal.

On top of everything else, you're not sure if what you feel is real. Maybe you made it up in a half sleep one cold night with a pillow over your head—like all those love letters with a billion promises of things "we're going to do when I get home"—you know. But you and your loved one are not soap opera stars. Much of what you put in those letters was serious, well-intended fairy tales. It was an image of what you *want to be*, not what you really are. It's a way of holding on to one another in a sick, unnatural state. Each of you tried to say what you thought the other wanted or needed to hear in order to keep your love alive.

But NOW, **it's show time**! It's a hell of a shock to come home to your "soul mate" and snap to the fact you are total strangers. You have to learn all over again to touch, be tender, close, and intimate. If this is a 100% jail house romance and the only place you've touched was in a visiting yard, both of you had better fasten your seat belts. It's going to be a rocky ride!

Like everything else, starting or re-starting an intimate relationship takes time, good intentions, patience, and humor. Frankly, if you jump right into bed, it is a critical error. First, you must build a bridge of tenderness and honesty in the real world that will support the weight of your years of heavy duty promises and concern. Get to know one another. Keep things light and easy. Go out and play! But do yourself a big favor: stay away from drugs and booze. You already have enough problems trying to get your head and heart together. Alcohol or drugs will twist every thought and feeling and make a hard trip simply impossible. Doing it right is the right thing to do.

Let me say it again: don't sweat the sex stuff. You have waited for *years*, so a few weeks (or even months!) of "romancing" isn't going to kill you. In fact, honest sharing of your feelings and fears can be much more intimate than anything your body can do. And never fear, it's like riding a bicycle; you never totally forget how! Plus, if you do fall off, it's not very far to the ground. Just remember: you are fresh out of a joint and your partner is scared to death. There is no way on earth all those sex-crazed fantasies in all those letters are going to actually happen. And if they do, it will be much later on. So don't damage this important relationship by trying to do the impossible.

While you were down you did one of two things: set the stage for the success of your relationship or set it up to fail. It all depends on how you approached it. If it was just a life raft, just a way to do your time, then you can do whatever you wish. It will end within a matter of weeks or months after you walk. If, on the other hand, your relationship has real meaning for you and you want it to work, certain things HAVE to happen both before and after release.

In the section **Personal Ties** on page 28, I stress the absolute need for a true friendship. This is the key that unlocks the draw bridge; it is the factor which turns mere illusion into something real and solid and good. In order to be true friends, you must learn to get close to each other without getting lost and surrendering your identity. You must be separate individuals even while sharing your love. This is VERY hard for "love junkies" to relate to. Believe me, I know. I used to fall in love with total strangers on elevators between floors!

In order to develop a relationship that will give us closeness *and* room to be ourselves, we must learn how to **bond** without **abandoning** ourselves. Then we can let down our defensive walls and get close to another person without destroying our relationship or ourselves in the process. The ability to balance self with others is one of the true secrets to a quality life. Once we have learned to do it, we will also have a greater ability to build new, fresh relationships with the people we meet in daily life. And we will make wiser choices about when to let down our bridge and who we let into our heart.

How Big Is Your Monkey?

> *"After being clean for three years I didn't think using would be a problem when I got out. But the very first party I walked into blew that illusion all to hell."*

I remember a dude in a north Louisiana jail saying his drug habit was like Godzilla when he just HAD to stomp a few towns. Almost all of us are addicts in one way or another. Some "jones" are minor, some super heavy...but they all eat our lunch if given half a chance. Usually our dependencies are the weakest links in our lives, the place where we are most vulnerable. Anyone wanting to leave the criminal justice system behind needs to honestly answer the following question: was my arrest and captivity a result of an obsession that drove me to surrender control of myself?

If so, the path to success will require us to do battle with that addiction. Addiction, by its very nature, takes control of what we do. It can be so powerful we come to believe it has its own personality and strength apart from us, but this is not true. In fact addiction is part of the way we think! It's something *inside our heads* that we embrace to meet the demands of daily life, something we depend on to help "take the edge off." But it never gives us true relief. The price we pay for cheap thrills and quick relief is the energy we need to have a richer life.

Often we think such things as drugs, sex, alcohol, or gambling are our problem, but that's not true. Our real problem is whatever drives us to **surrender** to mood-altering behaviors. Whenever you find an action, item, feeling, or person you "can't live without," that is a clear danger sign! Take a close and honest look to see if your behavior is based on a positive choice or a negative obsession. **Nothing** in life should have so much power that we cannot enjoy life without it! The question is: "What can we do about it?"

Life Without a Crutch

> *"So what if booze and crack do fry my liver and turn my brain to rust? Everybody has to die of something!"*

For me and thousands of ex-cons I've known, **nothing** is more deadly in the free world than being lost in one or more dependencies. Although we **know** something is uncool, we often hold fast to our ways even if it kills us! Coming out of prison puts a lot of stress on a person. When emotions and events overpower us, we may seek relief from dope, a bottle, extreme sexual activity, hurting people, etc. But the cold fact is that drugs, etc., don't solve our problems. They only *delay* them for a very short period. The problems are still right there the next day, just waiting to pounce on us! Coming out of a joint is the time when you need every little bit of yourself to cope and grow. The very **last** thing you need is another drain on your limited energy and resources.

So look within yourself and find your pocket of addiction. If you can't function without a cup of coffee, smoke two packs of cigarettes a day, are obsessed over some person, have a serious eating problem, get lost in sex books, etc., it's time to do something about it! What is the goal here? **Freedom!!**

You do NOT have to be a slave to a craving that destroys your dignity and self-worth! The idea that "once an addict, always an addict" is a cop out! You can learn to control and re-direct your mind and body. You may not be able to do it alone, but you *can* do it—that's a fact! Deal with it!

The burden is on you. Overcoming an addiction takes a lot of courage and hard work. It also takes a lot of help from people who understand what you're struggling with. Once you admit your problem, there is help available; you just need to reach out for it.

There is a book entitled *Life Without a Crutch* (see inside back cover) that can aid you in understanding the power of addiction and finding help to overcome it. If you do nothing else to prepare yourself for future success, **read this book!**

OVERCOMING MAJOR BARRIERS

Half In, Half Out

*"Even though my mind knows I'm out, something inside me
is still in that cage and it hasn't been able to shake free!"*

If you've never lived it, it is impossible to explain what it's like to re-enter society right out of prison. Some compare it to waking up after a hundred-year sleep. First, you appreciate a lot of small things that others take for granted. One example is **privacy**, just being able to be alone, quiet, away from the endless noise and presence of others. And it's truly grand to be able to come and go as you need and want to. Even a walk in the park can be a real joy! So let it all soak in.

If you've spent five years surviving in a prison, then right after you get out it's natural to think and talk about your life behind bars. At first prison memories and war stories are all you have to share with others. This is okay except that it blows most folks slam away and brings conversation to a dead stop! So try to grow more aware every time you do it and chill out whenever possible. Until you get over this, practice making "small talk" based on daily affairs. Even if this does seem sort of dull to you at first, that's where squares' heads are at! Use your insight, but spare folks the details of how and where you learned it.

Just as the adjustments into prison came in steps, so does return to the free world. A common and deadly trap for ex-cons and their families is trying to *rebuild overnight!* It's like thinking you can go from an empty lot to a skyscraper in a week. Lots of stress comes from expecting a magical, instant way to make everything wonderful. The longer you have been down, the longer it takes to put the puzzle together. In fact, for a long time after release, you don't even know what the pieces look like or how to find them. Some of the pieces you need may not even exist. In this case, it can take you years to learn to make them. So you can't expect to feel comfortable in the world for quite a while. You need to be patient and determined to find your way out of the maze!!

Don't try to catch up on what you've missed; it cannot be done. You cannot re-live the time you've lost, any more than you can capture a river in a bucket. All of life is ahead of you but it will come in small bites. Trying to "get it all now" is impossible. If you eat too much, your system cannot handle it. You just end up vomiting all over yourself. Be sure to study *99 Days & A Get Up* (see inside back cover) to get a good grip on the pace of your adjustment.

It normally takes a year or two before a person is more "here" than "there." It will depend on how much time you did, how old you are, and what came down during your stay. It takes a long time partly because the trip is so intense and because you have to slowly build a new way of living. With time and work, prison becomes the past, just old history, as it is replaced with new, fresh being. The best way to put the pen behind you is to reach out into the world for positive energy, replacing the old with the new.

If, after a few years, you find that your mind is "still in the joint" or your anger continues to take control, be smart and seek professional counseling to help heal the wounds. If you don't, your out-of-control emotions will endanger you, your bond with those you love, and possibly even your freedom.

The First Six Months

"When you get out, life is like a roller coaster running wide open! There is no way to get off so you grit your teeth and hold on!!"

The first six to nine months after release are WILD! It's like being on a roller coaster running out of control. All you can do is hang on for dear life. This is true both for ex-prisoners and for those who have awaited their return. This period is full of turn arounds, unexpected confusion and depression, childish delights, social rejections, and strange surprises. Many of the things you count on happening don't come to pass. And all too many things you prayed would miss you will come down on you like a load of bricks!

So this is a time for rapid adjustment of your hopes and plans. You can help keep your balance by taking pleasure in your new-found liberty and re-discovering some of the joys of just being alive! It's also useful to do *daily attitude checks* to keep yourself on target. Look for problems, like unloading your emotions onto other people during stressful moments. Also give yourself credit for the progress you've made. Stay flexible and ready to adjust your plans. Don't let any problem overwhelm you or push you into dangerous behavior.

If you hold your feelings inside, you will finally explode. So do all you can to communicate what you think and feel to the people you care about. This doesn't mean having an outburst of negative emotions or complaining about your problems day after day. But it is critical to your well being that you express your feelings honestly and openly. You may believe you're so different that no one can understand you, but you will find that people can often accept your sincerity and listen without passing judgment.

Also keep a sharp eye on how you treat those around you. It's not unusual to try to manipulate people or use the force of your body or will to keep them in line. This might have worked in the joint, but it is sure defeat when you're trying to make or keep friends. You know you don't like to be used and abused. In fact, you view anyone who does so as an enemy. You can be sure that other people will feel the same way if you try to lean on them. And in case you don't know it, you need all the friends you can get!

Coming home can be very wonderful or quite deadly. Be careful not to bounce out of the pen into an addiction or emotional dependency (not just drugs or booze, but other extremes such as getting married your first week on the streets to someone you just met). Any of these escapes will end up becoming a new prison. And don't be shocked that many things have changed ("Wow, there used to be a 20-story building here!"). Most ex-cons who have been down five years or more cannot believe how fast things move out here; so it's smart to kick back, watch, listen, and learn.

Most people feel very helpless during the first six months to a year, but that will pass. You will get knocked down many times; this is a normal part of life even if you haven't been to jail or prison. It's okay just as long as you keep getting back up! It takes time, courage, and lots of work to make life as good as it can and should be. Every time things get *really* strange, just say to yourself, "At least I'm not in the joint!" No matter how rough it is at first, never doubt that you **can be a winner**!

Priest or Pirate?

"I felt as though the word 'CON' was branded right between my eyes for the whole world to see."

Anyone who has been convicted of a crime and sent to prison will have a negative social image, and this often leads to rejection on many levels. There are lots of citizens who will refuse to have anything to do with a "criminal." Being denied a job or a chance to grow just because of your record can be very frustrating. But no matter how much being rejected hurts your feelings, you need to learn to blow it off. Remember that fear and mistrust come with the rap sheet; they won't go away overnight just because you want them to.

We all know that people are quick to judge others. But don't let other people's opinions shake your sense of your own worth. Often their views are based on what they were taught as children, on cultural values, or selfish interests. They may be right and they may not. Your actual worth is based on your character and the results of what you think and do. Nothing more and nothing less.

It is better if people throw flowers at you rather than stones. Better they call you hero rather than heel. But no matter how others see you, the real issue is how you actually behave, in thought and action. Therefore, the only accurate labels are those which reflect the facts of your behavior. If you lie, you are a "liar." If you tell the truth, you are "an honest person." So your best chance of being defined as "a good person" comes from doing good deeds. Even if no one else is aware, the person who best knows who and what you are is YOU.

Getting Pushed Around

"Everybody thinks they're running something—but usually it's nothing but their mouths!"

Day in and day out we interact with people. It's a give-and-take world. But let's face it: there are going to be a lot of people who oppose you or refuse to give you your way. This is nothing new. After all, you've been treated like a robot for years. But now you are on the streets and feel you should be "free" to run your own show and have things your way.

However, this is not always a simple matter. Ex-cons often come out of prison resenting *anyone* who tries to exercise power or authority over them. Many former prisoners walk around with a huge chip on their shoulders, quick to take offense at anything or anybody who resists their whims. In fact, we often overreact with strong emotions to situations that the average citizen deals with in a calm, effective way.

How you respond to "authority" and "people who just say NO" will have a *major* impact on your welfare. Automatic, get-in-their-face resistance to all external controls can be a real problem. After all, some authority is reasonable and must be dealt with. And, in most cases, the way people react to you is not a personal rejection of you but a simple response to the limits of reality. For example, an agency counselor cannot give you something he or she does not have or something that doesn't exist in the community.

So how do we tell the difference between "authority" which is reasonable and valid, as opposed to "resistance" which is unreasonable and just plain silly? Second, how do I, as an ex-convict, deal with being abused or intruded upon by idiots—the fools and jokers of the world?

To begin with, we expect to cope with reasonable authority figures such as our parole officer, employer, teachers, or certain family members. And there are people with whom we share authority and decisions, like our mates and friends. There are also people, like store clerks or phone operators, who are "just doing their jobs," even if we don't like the results. But we shouldn't have to put up with some rude parking lot attendant who *thinks* he's running something. Still, before you jump out and bite this fool's ear off in front of a dozen witnesses, ask yourself a few questions. First, are you *really* responding to the present situation or to something in your past? Is it in your best interest to get in this guy's face over trivial stuff? Is this really a valid issue or are you just looking for an excuse to unleash your anger? Are you exercising control over yourself? And, to be blunt, are **you** being a bigger idiot than he is?

No matter how we feel about a situation, we must stay cool enough to recognize what's really happening and react in a suitable way. By "suitable," I mean matching someone's action with our best possible reaction. A *suitable reaction* is one which leads to the most positive and constructive results. In order to react suitably, we must be in control of our minds and emotions so that we can identify the best available outcome and choose the most effective actions to achieve it.

Remember that a lot of "little people" huff and puff just to feed their egos. It's like that in the joint and can be even worse on the streets. Dealing with a teen-age drunk who thinks he's Superman, as an example, is nothing but a pain! But you *must* remind yourself that it isn't worth the price of a skinned knuckle to show him he can bleed. So be very careful: don't take everything personally! You don't have to act as absurd as he does. Let him find somebody who hasn't *been* to prison yet to blow him away! You have FAR more important things to do. It really helps to remind yourself over and over that you are not responsible for what others do. But you **are** responsible for how you react to them. Be the one sane person in a world of crazies!

Frankly, I found it very hard to put up with such trash. During my first five years out, I got into more than a few wrecks that could have put me back behind bars for life. But I can see now that I was walking around with personal problems *much* bigger than the petty stuff people laid on me. In short, I was searching for an excuse to explode. And as you know, if you go looking for trouble, you will find it or it will find you.

GETTING SETTLED

18 Months - A House of Cards

> *"Everything was going great! Then, without warning, my car blew up, my lady moved out, and I got fired for missing work...all in the same week! It seemed like I was better off in the joint."*

For the first couple of years after release, everything is very fragile. Any big wind can come along and blow you away. Just about the time you get on top of your basic survival needs and think you've got something going for yourself, **KA-WHAM**! One little thing will go wrong and suddenly your house of cards comes tumbling down!

This is a dangerous time. You haven't had a chance to save any resources to fall back on, so it's easy to be washed away. This is one reason ex-cons have to keep their game as tight as possible and not be shocked when one day, for no apparent reason, the bottom seems to fall out. I've watched it happen to me and many hundreds of people. Just keep in mind that it's all part of the maze; *everyone* has to live through it in one form or another. Despite the letdown that comes, this is just another step, another phase.

It may seem that you're suddenly back where you started; you may even wonder "why bother?" But that is just the mood of the moment. It will pass. Think of it as a *test* of what you're made of. In fact it is a **temporary setback**—certainly it's NOT the end of the world. The only danger is if you give up and refuse to rebuild what you've lost.

In truth, by now you have a lot more going for you than when you hit the bricks, so *just pull it back together and keep cooking!* Don't let anything break your heart at this critical moment. This is part of your dues—reality teaching you not to depend on your possessions or anything beyond your control. You haven't lost *yourself*, so **deal with it**! The goal is to come out a bit wiser so it doesn't happen again.

24 Months - Facing the Unexpected

> *"My past and my future were like two people in the same skin. And they were total strangers!"*

Two years or so have passed since exit. By now you can clearly see that much of what you focused on while down and right after release was simply wishful thinking. Since then reality has stomped your head in a few times and shown you how blind you were coming out of the joint.

This is especially true with *romances*. Like many people, you may have used a relationship to keep you going while in prison and help you get a fresh start in the streets. But now your illusions are fading, attitudes are shifting, and you may feel trapped. You may want to stay but feel you need to go. You hunger for security, but you also burn to be free to ride the midnight winds. Things feel very strange but you can't put your finger on why or what to do about it.

At this point, many people are torn between the influence of the past and hopes for the future. We often try to "pull up," to find some stability and quality of life we've never had. At the same time we don't feel comfortable with our new ways; we're not really sure we fit into a good-citizen role. So we stay in touch with our old ways—trying to keep a foot in both worlds. But we don't have enough energy, time, and resources to go forward *and* backward at the same time. When we try to go both ways, we cancel ourselves out and end up standing still!

Try to stay stable during this confusing time. You are not the old person you used to be and you aren't yet the new person you want to become. You are in between, which makes you feel a lot of stress and even guilt. Calm down and look within yourself to get a clear picture of who you are *today* and what steps you need to take *tomorrow*. Don't get hung up on who you used to be, what you don't have yet, or what you wish the future to hold. Take care of the business that's right in front of you. And think carefully before you make any decisions about major changes in your life. You don't want to build your future on what could be a passing whim.

If you think you're going to blow it, get help to sort things out, to work through this period of confusion. And I don't mean by consulting a fifth of Jack Daniels or a lid of sinsemilla. Look for someone you respect who can see things more clearly than you; it will help you get your balance back. As you go through your growing pains in the streets, it's natural to hit the wall at times. What is important is that you learn to handle it in a way that results in progress and pride!

30 Months - Critical Choices

"You make your own heaven and you make your own hell."

It's been about 30 months since release and lots of good things have come together. You have lived through the shock of release, pulled together your basic survival needs, overcome some major hassles, sorted out a lot of conflict, and begun to feel a part of the world. Great! You've come a long way, paid a high price, and have good reason to feel pride. Now it's time to confront a real moment of truth that will make or break you.

In prison all you wanted was to SURVIVE and GET OUT. After release all you wanted was to SURVIVE and STAY OUT. Things were hard but clear: you had to cope! Now that you are not totally driven by the after-shock of prison, you face some *critical choices*.

Daily life begins to place more and more petty burdens on you: stuff like car repairs, taxes, and school clothes for your kids. There is no place to hide. Your fate rests in your hands. You handle it or it eats you. No more promises to your family, parole officer, or yourself. Excuses don't cut it. Where you are right now is where you've said for years you wanted to be: in charge of your fate. Every day offers a crossroads: "In-Control Land" to the right, "Out-of-Control Land" to the left.

What is it going to be? Look life straight in its bloodshot eye, or retreat into chaos? What's your choice? At this point some folks are still trying to play both sides of the fence. But they become increasingly spread out, way too vulnerable. It only takes one slip-up and you're screwed. While other people can afford to waste their lives and send themselves to hell, *you have already been there!* Take advantage of the dues you've paid. Make a commitment to do **whatever it takes** to have maximum control over your life.

No matter which road you take, each has its own set of risks and rules. But before you choose the outlaw side, make yourself REMEMBER. Look back at how it feels to be chained up and treated like gorilla snot. Recall how it felt when your best friend turned state's evidence against you. Keep in mind how your father died while you were down and you couldn't even go to the funeral. And next time you slip, you might run the risk of catching life as a habitual criminal.

Ask yourself, "Is there anything in the pen I need to go back to learn? Did I miss something last time around?? Is there any future in playing the outlaw role? Do I want to die in a cage?"

Don't let anything or anyone distort your vision. Being responsible for yourself is hard work—VERY hard—and often not very exciting. But each new day that you make the choice to control your life is a step away from slavery toward freedom. You have earned your pride and self-respect, because you are making *great* progress. **Don't give up**!

36 Months - The Three-Year Itch

> *"When you finally get the Man's boot off your neck, you tend to go crazy with relief. I got real cocky and was ready to take on the whole world."*

There is something about being out about three years that is very weird. It's probably a mixture of things. By now you have some really good stuff going for yourself and you are determined to get more out of life than just survival. Also, you have more energy and part of you is *bored to the bone*. Plus, you have begun to forget just how bad it really was to be a slave and treated like you're ugly and stupid. You may even be thinking that your success in the free world has made you invisible and invincible.

Be careful. *Keep yourself humble*—or something is going to come along and kick your butt loose from the rest of your body. And that's an absolute fact! Dig it: *being free does not mean you can run loose and loud.* Around the three-year mark, one of two things happens: you get a close call that leaves you breathless, dizzy, and thankful. **OR** you go down again (prison, nut house, hospital, graveyard, whatever). No kidding, when you catch yourself getting real bold and starting to run hot, watch out. You're riding for a fall.

Settle down now and be very, *very* careful. You've come too far and paid too high a price to blow it over some nickel-and-dime trash. This is a time to hold your head up, do everything you can to make *good choices*, and finally realize that in fact **you can make it**! The best way to avoid the three-year trap is to take a deep breath, re-dedicate yourself to personal growth, and focus your extra energy on turning your dreams into reality.

You have made excellent progress! The secret here is to put your growing energy and intensity to greater and greater use. Continue to seek better ways to handle yourself, both in thought and action. Branch out into more educational, social, and cultural activities in your community. Take a night class, study self-defense, take up a new hobby, improve your job skills. This is a very sensitive time: *keep on moving forward!*

40 Months - Don't Rock the Boat

> *"Do not be consumed by your own fire! Settle down, keep your balance, and begin to really enjoy your freedom."*

By now you have successfully endured the major hardships of life after prison. You should feel a lot of satisfaction, because you've held onto your commitment to make it happen. You've made a big investment, and you can actually taste and touch the positive results. At this point, you don't want to lose it—it feels too damned good! You NEVER had that when you were ripping and running! You know now, without question, that what you want and need is in the free world, not in a concrete zoo.

I'll be the first to admit that the so-called "free world" leaves a LOT to be desired, but **keep your vision clear**! No matter how dull and dumb square life may seem, it *has* to be better than laying up on Christmas Eve in an ice-cold tomb of concrete and steel. Living a solid, productive, rewarding life doesn't mean you have sold out. You've simply wised up to the fact that your life is what you make it.

By now you *know* there are trade offs you must make for the things you want and need; everything has a price. Clearly a lot of sweat is required to put up with the endless details of daily living. But you also have proof that taking control of your welfare really pays off. You don't work on blind faith anymore. So when you get discouraged, sit down and have a heart-to-heart talk with yourself. Just look at the progress you've made—**just look**! Your efforts have earned you a new life of freedom and self-reliance.

Still, you sure are sick of the CONSTANT ups and downs of the roller coaster you've been on. You want more stability, even though stable living may not fit into your picture of yourself. Some hot shots might think the idea of being "stable" is just plain silly. But not you—you've been rebuilding your life from scratch and you *know* better.

Over the years since release, you haven't just been sitting in a dark corner, playing a dull, square game. Not at all! You are not the same person who hit the streets confused, frustrated, and angry. You have been living, growing, meeting new people, expanding your mind, discovering the world as never before. And along the way there have been rewards—events and feelings which have encouraged you and given you reason to persist against all odds.

You've come a long way; you've earned the right to have more stability and comfort in your life. And the way to put it there is to continue growing. By this time you know a lot about what you want in your life, work, and relationships. So keep working to improve in these areas! *Focus* your energy on getting yourself where you want to be. Improve your job skills so you won't be the first to get laid off. Set up a savings plan so that when something goes wrong it won't knock over your whole deck of cards. Work on solving problems in your relationships before they blow up in your face.

At the same time, you must realize that stable living does not mean things will always stay the same. No matter how stable you are, change will still occur. This is just the way life is. You can control some of the shifts but not all. So to find stability, you must improve your ability to deal with the unexpected curves that reality throws at you. Your greatest source of stability will be your calm confidence that you can cope with any obstacles you run into.

So think positive, hold your head up, and take another step forward. Be proud of what you have built, have faith in what you are going to achieve—and be thankful you are not going to die in a solitary cell with nothing but roaches for friends!

48 Months - Couch Potato Boogie

"When you don't have to be lean and mean any more, it's real easy to kick back and get fat!"

You never wanted the experience of going to prison or having to build a new life after you got out. Thus everything you've done so far has been out of **sheer necessity**. Looking back over the last four years, you will see a long path of efforts just to endure.

But mere survival is not the issue anymore. You have done a great job of dealing with the panic and crisis that came with life after prison. Now that the edge is off and the memory of the pain has eased up, many people are tempted just to coast. And if you aren't careful you can turn into a big, fat, lazy slug! Beware: *life doesn't stop here!*

There's no reason to simply settle for life in a rut—even a comfortable middle-class rut. Having what it takes to get by isn't enough! The new challenge is to protect all that you have built and keep moving forward. It's time to reach for the next gear. From this point on, you can aspire to improved *balance* in your life and continued *progress.*

You are now very close to the door of the maze. Freedom is in sight! Recommit yourself to whatever it takes to break free from the past. Up to now, events have forced you to focus on surviving one crisis after another. Now the crises are more rare. For the first time you can afford to aim far more energy and attention forward than you do backward. But it's up to you to keep on pushing; you will have to supply the focus. Strive to keep your mind and actions steady while having the courage and dedication to advance into the unknown! Are you going to settle for just getting over the past, or will you use this as a wonderful chance to make your life the way you've always dreamed it could be?

Life in the world offers so many more choices than you had in prison **or** in the reconstruction period after release. But you need new levels of self-discipline and courage to make living truly full and rewarding. Surely you haven't struggled so hard just to become a beer-drinking, TV-zapped couch potato.

It seems strange that, just as you are at the point of victory, you need a fresh supply of strength and will power to keep from getting lulled to sleep by your own success! Now that you have something going for yourself, you also have something to lose. At this point every ex-con has a new choice: to make life sweet or to screw up big-time. You don't want to blow what you have already achieved, but beyond that...you **must** take full advantage of this chance to live life to the fullest. You have dedicated your life to finding this door to the future. Now it's time to open it and step through.

54 Months - Facing Your Demons

> *"That there is a devil, I have no doubt. But is it outside trying to get in, or inside trying to get out?"*

Your growth and maturity are calling on you to tackle the **causes** behind some of your life-long problems. These are issues that go back to your roots, perhaps to childhood—very deep concerns you've never had the time, motivation, or ability to confront. You are ready to move beyond a survival holding pattern, but you keep running into some old walls, *time after time!* You can no longer permit them to stand in your way. Achieving escape velocity demands that you face these long-term barriers.

These barriers are like a group of demons that have been chewing on us for as long as we can remember. Even before any of us became prisoners of the State, we were prisoners of our own fears, self-images, and patterns of living that strangled our quest for peace and happiness. Deep beyond our reach, these ghosts still haunt us, affecting our interactions with ourselves and the world. Each time we think we're ready to step forward into a new life, our demons hook into our guts and snatch us back.

You've arrived at a *very* critical point in your quest for freedom. No longer can you simply accept being blown with the wind. It is time to turn about and face the invisible forces which command you! This is your only hope for gaining mastery over your fate. You now have the opportunity to begin fixing major parts of yourself that have never, ever worked. Not just repainting the front door but re-leveling the very foundation of your being!

Such deep, hard work is best faced with the ongoing help of a professional counselor. This is *not* someone who will manipulate, control you, or mess with your head. A counselor is a guide who can help you look at your thoughts, feelings, and actions from a different perspective so that you can start to work through rather than around your past! *Here* is where you begin to give the word "freedom" its true meaning in your life. You don't have to be trapped in the past just because "that's the way things have always been." With courage, persistence, and guidance from a wise teacher or counselor, you can free yourself from past limits.

Although this may have seemed impossible before, your years of hard work and growth have made you much stronger, wiser, and more balanced. Therefore, it's time to get serious about mastering the forces which lead to *quality of life*. You may need to learn how to set reasonable limits on yourself and others, how to tell the difference between "enough" and "too much." You may decide your self-image as a loser needs to go. Or maybe it's time to overcome your guilt, fear, insecurity, or inability to love and be loved—whatever it is that has kept you chained to unhappiness and failure. This rebuilding of your own foundation is the most intense form of personal growth. Your progress has earned you the right to get past the icing and deal with the cake.

60 Months - A Five-Year Victory

"It has been a long, rocky road and I'm proud of the fact I stuck with it—even when I wanted to dig up my pistol!"

Every new day of freedom is a victory because each brings with it a new chance to grow and prosper! But some points of progress are more special and rewarding in our lives than others. When you hit five years of arrest-free living, it is time to celebrate BIG TIME! To get this far means you have cleared 75% of the hurdles to success. More important, you have, at long last, found the door to the maze. You've actually made it!

How do you *know* it has really taken place? Is there a crack of thunder? Do you get a letter from the President? Does somebody give you a new Cadillac convertible? Most important, what does it feel like to know you have finally fought your way out?

Each person will feel it in different ways. I can only share with you what I personally felt when it happened to me. The following is my word picture of the experience I had when I realized I had finally exited the maze. Perhaps it will help you understand why this is a goal worth working and waiting for.

"It had been a long, hot, nasty 4th of July! I was running northwest into a merciless New Mexico sun. Thirteen hours on the back of a 1946 Harley chopper with the old Knuckle engine puking oil.

"The traffic was horrid rolling up the slope of the southern Rockies. For miles I'd been stuck behind an old logging truck as it lumbered around tight mountain curves. The driver refused to help me pass, and I was blind with rage, determined to get around him or die in the process. As we started up a steep incline, I dropped into third and punched it. I roared past him and hit fourth just as I swooped over the crest.

"Suddenly the sky exploded into a vast sunset of untold power and beauty. A million muted shades from mauve to aquamarine stretched across the limitless sky. It took my breath away and I smiled way down inside. As the sun slowly settled into the horizon, the shadow of my bike reached out and danced among the fence posts along the road. The first cool, sweet breezes of evening brought a rush of well being that dissolved my fatigue, soothed my anger, and filled my heart with peace.

"At the bottom of the next valley, I pulled off onto a dirt road and shut down in a pocket of trees beside a small mountain lake. As my ears opened to the sounds of the forest, I could hear the chatter of birds seeking out their nests for the night. The water was a mirror, rippled only by the occasional strike of a small fish. Here, totally alone in this quiet, private spot, I understood that all the struggles and day-to-day hassles I had endured were just the price I paid for the joy and magic of this instant.

"I suddenly realized that it took all the pain and suffering of prison to make me who I was. It was all that madness and isolation that had prepared my heart for the majesty of this enchanted moment. This private peace was what I'd dreamed of for 10 years. Now here it was—and everything was *totally* OK. It was then that I KNEW for the first time I was truly a free man!"

THE REWARDS OF SUCCESS

Step Right Up

"Look within your heart for the key to your fate."

My purpose throughout this book has been to motivate you to walk through fire to achieve personal growth and, ultimately, five years of arrest-free living. Yet I have no special power to change the way you think and act: only you have that. All I can really do is appeal to your better judgment and desire to lead the best life possible.

Sitting at this computer 20 years down the road from you, I know that vague, square-John promises of better times will not alter your way of looking at the world. And just because I have learned to value life and my place in it doesn't mean I can convince you to do the same. At this instant, you may be starving for a way out of the pit...or you may accept being dirt on the sole of someone's boot. Either way, it is your right to choose. All I can do is point the way: *"Better Times— Step Right Up!"*

If, as you read this, you are still an inmate existing from moment-to-moment, you cannot even *imagine* what it's like to experience the rush of making it this far. It might be easier for you to understand how an astronaut feels being weight-less during a space walk than to imagine the type of freedom I'm talking about. So much time and distance may stand between you and this level of freedom that it seems like a cruelty joke to talk about being five years free!

This makes sense, because the whole trip from release to true freedom is a total unknown for you. You may have stumbled so many times in the past you think success for you is impossible. In fact, you may not have a clue as to what the hell I'm talking about!

For someone who has never experienced it, the rich rewards of a life full of freedom and achievement may be beyond imagining. How, then, do I convince you to invest your mind, body, and heart in something you cannot see, feel, touch, smell, or otherwise know? I can only hope that when I tell you how good I feel about the changes I've made in my life, you will believe that such powerful and rewarding changes can also occur in your life. What I am telling you can be *tremendously* important to your life and future.

Becoming an EX Ex-Con

"I refuse to have my FBI number on my grave stone!"

We were given the label of "criminal" when convicted of a crime. This neg-ative identity lead to public rejection and limited our opportunities in the com-munity. And it had an equally profound effect on the way we saw ourselves.

After years of isolation and ridicule, you may have bought into the idea that you really were a worthless reject, a pile of social garbage. As a result, long after your release you were still property of the government! But now, after five years of work, faith, and positive changes, you have grown to see that your negative self-image is just useless baggage that keeps you a prisoner of the past. At this point in your life, you can shed the label of "criminal" like a snake sheds its skin. Look at the strides you've made, the lessons you've learned. You are not the same person who fell out of the joint five years ago! By now you not a "criminal" or "ex-con," but simply a "human being."

Being a convict is a tragic waste of time and energy. Why would anyone want to hang onto the experience and die an "ex-con"? Granted you still have a crim-inal record, but that is an external condition, not an identity. You don't have to accept the idea that you are some kind of social trash. *Never forget* that you can outgrow past mistakes. You do this by slowly replacing "criminal" thoughts and acts with health, growth, and prosperity.

The only way to really beat the system and become TRULY free is to let GO of a negative past and embrace a positive future! You are well on your way. Focus all your energy on making the future rich, full, and **free**! It can be done and YOU can do it!!

Inside the Circle

"To be within the Circle of Life means coming into a sense of harmony with yourself, loved ones, community, and the whole of creation!"

The day of conviction, we were officially kicked out of the circle of social acceptance, labeled as *outcasts*, and exiled to the Land of Castaways. After that, many of us felt "alone to the bone," completely cut off, totally isolated. And the period of captivity encouraged us to take the next step into self-isolation, becoming a stranger even to ourselves! THIS is the ultimate trap of the maze. Therefore, one of the most important steps in leaving the maze is to renew our contact with ourselves and re-enter the circle of humanity.

When you first came out of the joint, you may have seen the world as "the enemy" and gone through a period of telling everyone to go straight to hell. Your attitude may have been, "So they don't want me? Well, who needs 'um?!" If so, it was because your anger and hate prevented you from bonding with others or being part of the world you live in. But after you've been out five years, you have some real successes under your belt, most of all that you are still here in the free world. You have made many adjustments in order to get along in society and have some different ideas about who you are and what you want out of life. In fact, you are now a contributing member of the community.

But your awareness may lag behind reality. You may still feel an echoing emptiness surrounding you in the midst of a crowd. If so, now is the time to let go of that lone-wolf identity. You don't need it as protection any longer. You are a unique and important person who has made a place for yourself in the world. It is safe to start letting down your walls and re-connecting with the people around you. This is a gradual process and one that is different for each individual. If you don't know how to begin, that's a good reason to get some guidance from a professional counselor. You can use the help, not because you are sick, but because you are ready to get healthier.

At some point, you will find you just don't need so many defenses anymore. One day you will simply realize that there is a gateway through your walls and you have the key. Maybe it will come to you in the quiet way it came to me.

"In prison I pulled back, totally and completely, from everyone and everything. I identified with the label "single O," a loner's loner. For many years this condition continued in the streets. No matter where I was, who I was with or what we were doing, I was alone! My isolation was my shelter—and my tomb. The hard part was learning to trust!

"Gradually I met some truly fine people, especially my wife, and over time began to feel more comfortable, more 'there,' when other people were around. Last week we had some people over for dinner. As we sat around the table, it hit me that I was part of the group—I actually fit! I wasn't just sitting back watching what was happening; I was an accepted part of this circle of friendship. It was like a great weight was lifted from my back, as though my soul could finally breathe. Far more than just being out of prison, I was truly home!"

Life Beyond the Maze

"Instead of just living day-to-day, it's time to get ahead of the game."

Up until now most of your energy has been spent trying to overcome your past and exit the maze. Survival and damage control have been the major concerns. In short, most of your attention has been on what you're moving away *from* rather than what you're moving *to*. Now, with most survival issues in check, you can look *forward*, into the **future**! More and more you can let go of the past and shift your attention to new, fresh ways to think and live.

What awaits you on the other side of the maze? As you shift into higher gear, you begin to reap some of the rewards for all your years of serious work, faith, and patience. At this point you can begin to pursue some long-term goals that will bring you greater stability and tremendous satisfaction. Shop the fall sales for things you'll need next spring. Plan for the overseas trip that you once lay in a cell and dreamed about. Look at what it will take to buy a house rather than just renting. Think about what you would need to do to pursue a career change or to start your own business. Now is the time to look at your truly long-range plans and decide how to make them real.

And as you continue to improve your own life, also think about what you can do to improve the world around you. As long as you were fighting to survive, you didn't have anything left over to share with the world. You couldn't give what you didn't have. But now you have some physical, financial, and emotional security. Granted it's not what you want it to be yet, but you can now afford to give a little of yourself to the welfare of others. You also have personal skills, a great deal of insight into life, and a very powerful ability to focus your energy on a goal and make it happen. These are talents that can make a positive difference in your community.

So consider dedicating some of your resources to solving problems that are greater than your own life. Find an issue that needs work and means something to you, and decide to help make things better. This commitment to making the world a better place may be the most rewarding thing you have ever done. I know it has been for me.

Please keep in mind that the more you apply and focus yourself, the more power and control you will have over yourself and everything around you. This will lead to ever greater security, comfort, and quality of life, and to honest self-respect. Now that you have reached this point of achievement, you don't have to walk around looking at the ground anymore. You can look up into the stars! Freedom, progress, and pride are no accident; *you've earned them!*

ADVICE FOR FAMILIES OF OFFENDERS

by Louis W. Adams, D.Min.

Being the family member or the loved one of a public offender results in countless problems and burdens which no one wants or is born knowing how to handle. Many social, emotional, spiritual, and financial difficulties arise when you become involved in the criminal justice system. At times, you may feel lost in these difficult and unexpected concerns.

In order to cope, it helps to know some of the basic problems and universal experiences people face during the correctional experience. One encouraging fact that aids survival and growth is the predictable nature of the experience. Many of the events and resulting challenges affect almost everyone who becomes involved. Although knowing what is to come does not make it simple or easy, it does improve your preparation and increase your confidence to handle the events in the most effective way possible.

DEALING WITH LOSS

"The day of sentencing a big part of me died."

Family members and loved ones of persons caught up in the criminal justice system are going to have many of the same experiences the offender does. But they are also called on to endure feelings and events unknown to the inmate. While some of these emotional and social changes are similar to things people face in daily life, others are unique to the correctional process. At the heart of these experiences is one central issue, *the sense of loss.*

Personal Factors

First, you lose the physical presence and daily contact with the incarcerated person. Even though you may not have approved of his or her behavior, you were used to their presence and it comes as a shock when they suddenly vanish. He or she is no longer around to support you or "bug" you, as the case may be. You lose your personal interaction with that person. It may even feel as though a part of your body has been cut away.

You also lose the role he or she played in the family and other groups to which he or she belonged. That role might include financial, emotional, and/or spiritual contributions the loved one made through normal daily activities. Even if the person had become a drain on you, you will still miss having him or her involved with you from day to day.

Second, you have probably lost the person you always believed your loved one to be. You may have often said to him or her, "You will end up in big trouble if you don't change what you're doing." But you *still* believed and hoped that something would change before your loved one really did get into trouble. His or her arrest, conviction, and imprisonment destroyed this belief and hope!

Your belief and hope have often been a very important part of your own values, goals, and expectations. Having them come to an abrupt end is experienced as a deep and painful "loss," a major event in your life. No one is ever really ready to confront such a "significant loss." It will be felt as a loss even though the overall situation with the loved person has not been perfect or really satisfying. And when you experience a loss as "significant," it is natural for you to grieve that loss.

Grief Is Natural

When a loved one is incarcerated, grief is a natural, human response. It includes any or all of a series of feelings which must be accepted and dealt with. The order in which these feelings are experienced may vary with each person.

The first feeling most people have is *shock*. It may be sensed as an absence of feeling, a kind of numbness or emptiness, rather than a sharp feeling like anger, betrayal, or pain. You may feel as if something is gone from your gut, like there is a hole there; you may feel light-headed; you may feel that you are not quite connected with your immediate world; or you may feel a combination of all of these. The onset of such feelings can be very disturbing. If you don't have any of the above reactions, you may feel nothing at all, and this absence of feeling can also be upsetting.

Confusion often follows or comes with the initial shock. But don't let the confusion, the absence of feeling, or the onset of strong negative feelings distort your sense of reality. This kind of reaction is not unusual; it is quite natural. Parts of the body, mind, or emotions sometimes shut down for awhile. This protects you from being overwhelmed by unexpected, traumatic, and dreaded events. In this sense, shock may be helpful by acting as a temporary shield to protect you.

You may also defend against a trauma by trying to *deny* that the terrible event happened. This *often* occurs while you are in the state of shock. For example, when you first learn of your loved one's crime or incarceration, you may deny (or fervently hope) that what has happened simply isn't true. You keep hoping you will wake up and find the dreaded event was only a dream (well, maybe a nightmare). You may, against all evidence, continue to hope that it is all a giant mistake. But you will not wake up! It is not a mistake. What happened really *did* happen and you will have to accept it as true.

A state of shock does not usually last very long. But the denial of what happened may go on for days, weeks, months, or in some cases for years. No matter how natural or useful the denial is at first, you need to come out of the shock and denial. The sooner you can get yourself going again, the quicker you can start to be effective in handling your life and the situation you are facing.

Anger

"I just get so mad at the whole situation!"

Once the numbness and denial of shock have passed, it is very common for a person to feel *anger*, lots of anger! You may feel anger toward your loved one because his or her actions caused the pain and problems which you now have to face. The anger can be very intense, especially if your loved one ignored your warnings and pleading to stop what he or she was doing. Your anger may be directed toward the police, the courts, an attorney, or toward "them." You will probably feel anger at times toward any or all of these sources, plus others.

Having angry feelings toward things and people outside yourself has its own set of problems with which you must deal. But anger is not confined just to outside objects or other persons. There is a very high probability that your anger will be turned back on yourself—in the end if not at first. This is a form of guilt, a self-blaming process. You may tell yourself such things as, "If I had been smart enough, good enough, persuasive enough, strong enough, worked hard enough, had knowledge enough, or paid attention to the signs of trouble sooner, I could have prevented all this from happening."

While there can be some truth in these criticisms, none of them is totally true. It is not useful to go on criticizing yourself indefinitely. Whenever you get angry or overly critical of yourself, and keep these feelings focused on yourself for a period of time, *depression* will set in. This is a fundamental rule of the life process.

Depression

"I could hardly drag myself out of bed; if it hadn't been for the kids, I wouldn't have bothered. Some days, I never even opened the blinds."

Depression is one of the most difficult parts of the grief experience. It is hard because it uses up so much of your emotional, psychic, spiritual, and physical energy. You will likely feel very bad, drained of all energy and initiative. Or you may feel flat, or just plain empty and hopeless.

You will probably fuss at yourself about various "failures" you have had both past and present. For example, you may feel guilty and tell yourself that you did not do the "right things" to prevent your loved one from being incarcerated. You may have tried hard to correct the behavior pattern your loved one was following, but your efforts did not help.

You may feel you bungled and did not get him or her the right kind of help. You may feel that all of your decisions during this ordeal were wrong and that this is why your loved one is incarcerated and you are in so much pain. You may feel your total life is a failure; not only have you failed your loved one, you may also believe that you have failed as a person throughout your life. This feeling is especially common among parents of prisoners.

If you pay attention to these failure messages and come to believe them, your confidence in yourself may be badly shaken and undermined. If you lose confidence in yourself, you will probably doubt your ability to make good decisions. You may therefore avoid making decisions altogether. And this is not a time to quit making decisions, no matter how difficult your choices seem to be.

Another reason that decisions are hard to make is because you don't have enough energy. The energy you once used to make decisions is now being used to deal with the depression. You simply don't have as much energy available to deal with the normal tasks and decisions of everyday living, let alone deal with any major decisions about the incarcerated person and your own affairs. You may find that you don't make decisions as easily or as effectively as you once did.

Even simple tasks do not get done as easily or as well as before. You have only a certain amount of energy available to deal with all of life's tasks. So when you use more of your energy to deal with your depression, less will be available for doing all the other things you have to do, such as making decisions. Your efficiency in dealing with life will suffer.

When you notice that you are less efficient, you may start to doubt your ability to do anything well. This in turn may cause you to fuss at yourself for your lack of ability. If this happens you become more depressed and will doubt yourself even more. When you are caught in this depressed state of mind, everything around you can seem like quicksand. Every effort you make will seem to pull you down further into depression and ineffectiveness. You may even use this experience to prove to yourself that you are incompetent as a person.

At the same time, you will likely get more and more requests from your loved one to do things and solve problems. As these demands pile up, you will feel frustrated, and this can make you feel more depressed. You may get very tired and angry at the demands being made on you. No matter what you do, it seems to be not "enough," not "effective," not "right," or it turns out to be irrelevant or unnecessary. And when you do all these things for your loved one, you don't seem to have any energy left to do things for yourself.

When your anger and frustration reach a certain level, you will probably "dump" it. You may dump it on your incarcerated loved one, other family members, friends, your lawyer, the jailers, the judge, prison employees, the parole board or anyone else who happens to be handy. Of course, dumping anger and stress on others will not be helpful to you or your loved one. Neither will the added depression caused by the dumping. Often it just increases your own sense of frustration and helplessness.

Trying to endure levels of stress or pain beyond your limits can result in a physical or emotional illness. In this situation, you may feel so overwhelmed that you think you cannot hang on and simply want to give up! But this is not a positive solution; the situation won't go away even if you do give up. You will get greater relief by learning healthy ways to overcome depression and stress.

Other Feelings

Other feelings may also overcome you. You may feel *shame*, because your loved one has been labeled a "criminal." You may fear being *embarrassed* if co-workers or members of your church find out your loved one is in prison. And it is not uncommon for children of prisoners to be ridiculed by others at school or in the neighborhood. To make things worse, at times family members will reject other members because they continue to stand by an inmate. One or more of these things can cause you to isolate yourself from your friends or family.

You may feel guilt, because you didn't prevent this from happening or because you "failed" to inspire your loved one to be a better person. You might also feel guilty because, at first, you were relieved that the uncertainty of the pre-trial activities was over. You may tell yourself that feeling relieved when someone dear to you is incarcerated is just "not right." Along with all of the above, you will probably feel *frustrated and powerless* simply because you have little or no control over what is happening.

You may experience any or all of these feelings in any order or several at a time. You may feel *overwhelmed* with them and think you are really losing control of yourself—maybe going crazy. This can increase your anger and guilt because you view yourself as inadequate to handle the load.

Sometimes the situation gets too "heavy" to bear, and you will walk (or run) away from it. When this happens, it may that your mind and body are protecting you from an overload. Sometimes it is helpful to exit the stress of the moment and "hide" for awhile. This lets you recover your balance and your perspective. Then you can return to the battle refreshed.

Such an act does not mean you are a weak or bad person or that you are uncaring, disloyal, or selfish. If you choose to do this to get recharged, don't let anyone put you on a guilt trip for deserting the battle. It is simply one way you can survive when you have reached the outer limits of your endurance.

However, if this happens often, or you do not get back into taking care of essential "business" within a reasonable time, it is a sign of danger for your health and future. It is time for you to seek outside help because you are probably running away from things you will have to face at some point. Putting them off will not make them go away.

Sometimes the troublesome feelings may go away for awhile. You believe that you have, at last, gotten over your grief and depression. Then something happens, perhaps during a visit with your loved one, and the grief feelings return stronger than before. This too may make you think you're going crazy. Although very unpleasant, this not particularly unusual. Feelings may come and go many times during the course of your grief. Even as you begin to move back into a more normal life pattern, these feelings—especially periods of depression, anger, and apathy—may return.

When the depressed feelings are strong, you may decide that nothing is really important. You may not care about anything and may do little or nothing. In more intense moods of depression, you may feel life is not worth living and there is no use in trying. In fact, you may get to the point where you believe that nothing good can happen, either now or in the future.

Even after your life is almost back to normal and you seem to be coping well with all your problems, you may have a recurrence of these feelings of depression. Even if this happens to you several times, do not despair. There is hope!

FIGHTING DEPRESSION

Depression Can Be Overcome

"I didn't think I could ever enjoy going fishing without Henry, but I'm glad I tried it. I missed him, but I had a good time. And I felt more like coping with things when I got home."

Depression keeps you weak and helpless by telling you that you have no energy to do anything. It may cause your sleep to be disturbed so you feel even more tired. Your apathy may increase. Messages of hopelessness may become very, very strong and hard to resist. But do not give up! Depression can be overcome. It is not easy, but it is possible.

You start overcoming depression by making yourself do things even when you don't think you can. For example, you must make yourself go to work, clean the house, keep the car running well, spend time with other people. If you have trouble sleeping, do not lie in bed; get up and do those long-neglected chores you hate so much. After you do this once or twice, you may find you will go to sleep in order to avoid doing the things you hate to do!

Many people report that the hardest part of this task is making themselves do things that they used to enjoy doing. No matter how difficult this may be, *you must make yourself do it.* If you start doing these things and you make yourself get involved with caring people, you will be surprised to find that your energy has increased and your interest in life is vibrant again.

It is also important to stop doing things that aren't helpful or necessary, like smoking, drinking, overeating, neglecting personal appearance and hygiene, or second guessing all your decisions. Such activities have no benefit, either short- or long-term. Therefore, do not waste your precious energy on them.

Instead, do the things that take care of necessary business and help you relax. These will give you both short- and long-term benefits. Most people know what to do to take care of business, but often don't know how to relax. If you don't know how to relax, then now is the time to learn. Things that relax you may also be fun. After you learn them, be sure you don't block yourself from doing them. In our society, people often believe it is "bad" to relax and have fun when a loved one is in prison, sick, or in trouble. Purge your mind of this thought. It is not useful or helpful.

Part of any person's responsibility is to take genuine care of his or her own physical, mental, emotional, and spiritual health. Taking care of necessary business is fundamental to this task. But relaxing and having fun is also an important part of this responsibility. When you relax and have fun, your self-esteem and self-confidence will grow. You will feel refreshed and able to use your energy more effectively. And when you feel competent and confident in yourself, your help to your loved one will be more effective.

Protect Yourself

"I found myself doing time day-for-day with my son, but I got so miserable I was no help to him or me. I had to shake myself out of it or go under."

A prisoner cannot come and go at will nor participate in the events of daily life. But the fact that your loved one is locked up does not mean you should be cut off from the world as well. You are not the one sentenced to prison. It does the prisoner absolutely no good for you to sit in a corner and sulk and brood until he or she is released.

However, a prison inmate can be very selfish. Your loved one may, in fact, expect you to suffer and brood in isolation just as he or she does. An inmate may not understand that *you have the right to your own life*—a calm, happy, normal, and healthy life—even if he or she is unable to have one. The prisoner may not realize that your help will be more useful and effective if you are feeling confident and satisfied about yourself.

Don't be caught off guard if your loved one criticizes or attacks you for doing things for fun and relaxation. It is not unusual for an inmate to accuse you of not caring, of being unfaithful or disloyal, etc., because you have been doing something fun. Don't let such criticism throw you! There is no reason to feel guilty about it, even if your loved one tries to make you feel guilty. Remember, you must keep your own emotional, spiritual, mental, and physical health in good order. This will help you keep your self-esteem and confidence high.

Relaxation and fun are part of your most important task—**to take care of yourself**. It is absolutely essential that you accomplish this task. And ultimately, it is one of the most helpful things you can do for your loved one. There is *nothing* to be gained by staying locked in your grief and agony. If you are not keeping yourself physically, mentally, emotionally, and spiritually healthy, you will not be as effective in helping your loved one, no matter how hard you try.

Accept Your Limits

Do not expect too much of yourself; you are not super-human. A person whose loved one is incarcerated often feels responsible for relieving their misery or even for getting that person out of prison. While each of us has responsibility toward another, this does not include control of the way a person acts, thinks, or feels. Your loved one is finally and solely responsible for being where he or she is. *He or she ONLY is responsible—you are **NOT!***

It is true that your loved one can use a lot of help—during incarceration, when seeking parole, and after release. But this does *NOT* mean you can or should do *everything*. Remember that you do not have a magic wand with the power to "fix" everything. It is easy to pressure yourself into taking on more than you can handle or to do more for your loved one than is really good. In the end this will only deplete your limited resources and weaken the prisoner even more.

Keep this in perspective. If your loved one can do something alone, encourage and insist that he or she do it. It is particularly important for a prisoner to accept responsibility for his or her own growth and emotional stability. Don't let your loved one or anyone else put you on a guilt trip for failing to do what you cannot do, or for not doing things your loved one must eventually do for him or herself.

Likewise, you don't have the power to make the police, court, prison, or parole board take any particular kind of action. You might work hard to influence them, but they will ultimately decide what to do about your input. Expecting the criminal justice process to operate in a rational way or expecting too much of yourself and others will only increase your frustration. Therefore, do not feel guilty or responsible for the actions of these agencies. It will only keep you in grief and depression and decrease your usefulness to yourself and your loved one.

Keep a Good Attitude

It is also important to remember that what you are experiencing is a *natural* reaction. Everyone experiences loss and depression sometime in life, although the direct cause may be different than yours. It helps to know that what you are experiencing is natural.

There are other things that can also help. For example, never let depression lead you into feeling sorry for yourself. Never become a "poor me" person; this will just make you your own worst enemy. Realize that depression will pass if you work on it and if you let it pass.

Never become so friendly with depression that you decide you cannot live without it. Don't laugh: people do become dependent on depression and resist giving it up as if it were an old friend. Instead of befriending it, tell yourself the truth. You *will* live through this experience. You *can* feel again that you are a good, useful, and worthwhile person with a lot to offer others. You do not need depression as a friend. You can't afford it.

GET HELP!

If you have trouble with any of the things noted above, *do not hesitate to get help*. You can get support from friends, ministers, support groups, or other people who care. There are many sources of help available in most communities.

Sometimes your problems may be serious enough that you need help from a trained professional. You may need temporary medication to help you establish good sleep patterns or overcome intense depression. You may need a professional counselor to help you work through your grief or establish good coping patterns for the depression.

Aside from negative or crisis reasons, there is much to be said for seeking help for positive or constructive reasons. If the departure of your loved one demands major changes—whether economic, social, or personal—in the way you live, it is wise to seek help in finding job training, new types of employment, and new insights into yourself and your relationships.

Make sure you get help if you need it! There are many professionals available. If money is a problem, there are social service agencies that offer competent professional help for a low fee. Getting help from professionals can be part of taking good, genuine care of yourself. Never hesitate to seek the help you need. You deserve to have a calm, peaceful, and happy life.

Find a Support Group

Another important resource that can help you deal with grief and depression is a support group. For many of you, the church can fill this need. If faith and religion are important to you, or have been important to you in the past, it may be wise to maintain or re-establish your involvement with the church of your choice. This can be difficult if you feel you don't deserve to be a part of the church or that you have somehow let God down. Again, this is not an unnatural feeling, given the circumstances.

The church, however, has the potential to understand your plight and be a source of support if you give it a chance. You may hesitate to do this. You may feel the members will look down on you as a failure, as one who has fallen short of the goals of the faith group. Again, this could be true of some members of some groups. Most, however, will want to help.

Do not let your guilt, fear, depression, or anger keep you from reaching out for the help and support you need. Remember, most faith groups believe that "all have fallen short of the Glory of God." Chances are, if you don't "poor me" them to death, at least some members of the group will be willing and able to help you maintain your sanity and a healthy, realistic perspective on life. If you do not find support in the first place you try, try another church or faith group.

Even if faith and religion are not important to you, there are other groups in your community that can help you take care of yourself. Being part of a support group gives you the chance to help others who are also struggling with losses. Being with them in their struggles can help you work your way through your own struggles.

Knowing that you can help others and that your help is needed by others is good medicine for guilt, depression, and the other feelings associated with grief. If you have never been involved in any group outside your family or closest friends, it can be doubly important for you to join a support group. The group can be a great help to you and may be a good source of help for your loved one down the road. People do need help from each other; it is a natural and healthy process.

If you find that no such group exists in your area, you may wish to start one. This involves finding others with a similar need and then coming together to discuss issues of common concern. Many positive things, such as information sharing, car pooling, and emotional support, can take place in person and over the telephone. Don't sit in a corner and mope; reach out to others who understand and also need help.

YOUR RELATIONSHIP WITH REALITY

Grief and the Perspective of Reality

"Hopelessness is self-defeating. A negative perspective locks you into grief, frustration, anger and, ultimately, a hopeless view of the world."

What has been discussed so far deals mainly with what you experience—what you do and feel. Another element in grief is that of *perspective*. This refers to the meaning or interpretation you put on all the experiences discussed previously. For example, a person in the midst of grief may interpret everything that happens through the influence of depression or anger. In this case, interpretations will inevitably be negative, pessimistic, or even hopeless. That person will interpret even positive or neutral occurrences as negative.

For instance, a parole board's first review decides against your loved one. You might interpret this experience to mean something like, "They are just prejudiced against us. There is no use in doing anything different for the next review because it won't help." If this is your perspective, you will find "proof" of the board's prejudice, regardless of its decisions. If your perspective is negative, you can easily talk yourself or your loved one into avoiding contact with the board because "it will only be a waste of time." This is a hopeless attitude. A more useful and productive attitude would be, "Even if my loved one is never paroled, it may help to give the board information to support his/her parole chances."

It is not easy to deal with "set-offs and turn downs," to be told "you don't have the right person or the right office to deal with your request." When you experience these obstacles, it is very difficult to keep a positive attitude. And it can be especially hard when one bad experience follows another. To help keep your perspective, remember: the vast majority of people sent to prison are eventually released back into the free world, and many of them are released on parole.

A negative perspective may also affect your attitude about other difficulties in your life, for instance, problems at work or with friends. You may think that all of your problems are caused by having a loved one in prison or that there is no way to solve your problems because the world is against you. But these ideas are not true. Problems occur in everyone's life, and they can be endured and overcome.

While in the midst of grief, it is not unusual to have negative perspectives from time to time. The important thing is not to hold onto this perspective so long that you lock yourself into grief. To keep things in a clear and true perspective, remember that your experiences and reactions are natural. You are only being human, and it is normal for you to feel this way. Your main job is to get *through* the grief and not get "stuck" in it.

Social Factors

There is another common experience reported by many who have loved ones incarcerated. You may feel that other people are deliberately avoiding you or are always staring at you. Some people who know about your loved one's situation may stare at you and avoid you. But most people will not. Your feelings are likely a reaction to any shame you may feel.

You may believe that everyone will automatically condemn an offender and all his or her friends and relations. It is true that some people will judge you to be guilty by association, or guilty for failing to be a "good" parent, spouse, or whatever. Some of these people may even be family members or people you thought were your friends. But most friends and relatives will not automatically make these types of judgments. If they do judge you, there is probably nothing you can do or say to change their minds. It may be necessary and best if you simply stay away from them as much as possible.

If you feel a distance or coolness from friends or family members, it may not be because they are "judging" you or your incarcerated loved one. Often they may feel uncomfortable with you or your situation. In short, they just don't know what to say or do. And since they don't know how to respond to you, they hold back and try not to get involved.

You can often help them get over their reservations by being honest and displaying a "good attitude." Although there is no guarantee that you can change their response, keeping your sense of humor can be a great help. Humor can be found under almost any circumstances, no matter how grim. Showing that you still have a sense of humor in an awkward or grim situation can put others at ease. This frees them to be natural and supportive of you. Some good examples of the positive use of humor can be found in the TV series "MASH."

There are people who believe that showing humor under these circumstances is wrong, even sacrilegious. However, if humor can bring you to a clearer, more realistic perspective, and can free others to be supportive of you, I feel it cannot be bad or sacrilegious. So I urge you to find your humorous self, even in the midst of these very trying and unpleasant experiences.

People may also distance themselves from you if you wear your depression on your sleeve. This is especially true if you play "poor me" whenever they are around. Let's face it, "poor me" people are a real drag to be around. But, once you show them you are the same person they have known and that you have a sense of humor, they will likely become friendly and supportive.

Act natural and let your friends and relations know about your trouble, but don't press them about it. Once they are comfortable with you, some of them will prove to be a great help in working through your grief and depression. The people around you can help you keep a hopeful, realistic perspective on your life. And they are often *eager* to help.

YOUR RELATIONSHIP WITH YOUR LOVED ONE

Dealing with someone in prison is often difficult at best. For most people, the only regular means of communication is through letters and occasional visits. While these are not the preferred or most effective ways to stay involved with a loved one, they may be the *only* way. Therefore, you will use them. You will use them because it is important for your relationship that you keep track of what is going on with your loved one and share necessary information. Maintaining regular communication is extremely *important* to a person in prison, and to you as well. So write regularly even if your loved one does not.

Visits

A visiting room is frequently a crazy, loud, unnatural place to see or visit anyone, let alone those closest to you. There is little privacy, though some prison units have more than others. Without question, jails offer the least privacy. They often give a first time visitor a real shock. Your first reaction may be, "You've got to be kidding if you think I'm going to visit anyone here!" But this is the facility you must use, so try to get used to it. Plan each visit carefully, especially when there is business to transact. Time is usually limited, so use it well and wisely.

Never assume the visit will be good or bad. In reality you cannot predict what mood your loved one will be in. You might find him or her angry and hostile toward you, the jailers, the guards, the warden, other inmates, or the world in general. Or they may be depressed. They may play a good game of "poor me" with you.

Whatever happens during a visit, remember, a prisoner lives in a very unnatural world. A jail or prison is a gigantic container of hostility. Both staff and inmates tend to be hostile. Even though your loved one really looks forward to your visit, you still may get a great deal of hostility or depression dumped on you. Your loved one may be angry or depressed because of something that has happened in the prison. He or she may be angry or play "poor me" because you have not done something you were asked to do, even if the request could not or should not be done.

Often the emotions expressed by your loved one are not really directed at you personally. In fact, it rarely is your fault. Do everything you can to avoid taking the anger or depression personally. And refuse to respond in like manner. Visits are very short and you will soon be able to drive away, so be as understanding as you can.

Be Honest

Another cardinal rule about communicating with your loved one is to be honest and straight about your feelings and about everything you discuss. Above all, never hide anything from your loved one to "protect" him or her. It is most important for your loved one's future adjustment in society to face reality now. Never allow a false picture about what is really going on at home, about plans for release, or anything else. Your loved one may not need to know everything that is going on, but he or she does need to know what is fundamentally important.

Get Good Information

Be prepared for your loved one to tell you stories or pass on advice from other inmates. Such stories and advice may be totally false, or partially or totally true. Your loved one has no way to find out what is true or not true. You will dismiss a lot of this type information because it is clearly untrue. But some of the information will need to be checked for accuracy through other sources. You will have to do this for your loved one. But be discriminating; don't get hooked on trivial or irrelevant issues.

This advice also applies to the things your loved one may ask you to do. Often, their requests are impossible to do, or useless or unnecessary. Inmates can rarely learn the truth about stories or advice by themselves. You are the one who can find out what is useful and not useful, what is possible and not possible, what is necessary and not necessary, what is true and not true. Remember, an inmate does not live in the real world! *You are the chief source of contact with the real world and with truth.* Therefore, you need to have as much accurate information as possible about prison rules, parole regulations, appeals procedures, etc. ALL inmates suffer from false information and expectations; **you** must be prepared to help your loved one test reality.

You can't usually prepare in advance for the issues and requests your loved one brings up. But you can get the information after your visit and report your findings in letters. This is one reason it is so important to write regularly and often. Remember, you are the link with hope, reality, and truth. A big part of your job is to report the facts. Never underestimate the importance of this, even if your loved one has a negative reaction to your information.

Be Prepared

Be aware that a "bad" visit with your loved one or a "bad" letter may throw you back into the grief process after you thought it was over. This is not unusual. If you are rested, healthy, and prepared for ups and downs, you can keep the damage to a minimum. If you are working through the grief cycle, the feelings won't be as intense and they won't last as long as they did at first.

Your reaction to a bad visit or a complaining letter is a good way to tell how well you are dealing with your grief. If you fall back into depression, or if your attitude gets negative, apathetic, or overly angry, it is a sign you are not overcoming your grief. This is especially true if the bad feelings are as intense and last as long as before. In this case, you could probably benefit from some help. So, *go find it!*

Jail House Romances

"A treasure chest of love..or a life raft full of holes?"

Some of the personal or romantic relationships between inmates and free world people start or expand after the offender is sent to prison. In fact, new and very powerful ties may develop even when the individuals never knew each other in the free world. Such relationships are unique; they are "not of this world," but they seem to have a special magic all their own. It is like a person from Earth developing a close intimate relationship with a being from Mars.

Developing a long-distance relationship under such conditions can be very romantic, dramatic, and exciting. Each partner offers the best of themselves and hides the worst; each offers or promises what the other one wants (even if it doesn't exist). But these relationships usually lack the elements needed to be successful after incarceration. The partners thrive on fantasy and illusion. They make elaborate plans for the future, but their plans are built on sand and thus highly vulnerable to the tides of reality which follow release from prison.

To be brutally blunt, jail house romances make good melodrama but not good sense. Why? Because the factors needed to build a healthy, rewarding intimate relationship are unfortunately absent. This does not mean that two people should not care about each other. They can communicate deeply and share time and energy together. But they should not exceed the bounds of reality. If they do, they set themselves up for great disappointment, grief, anger, and depression when they meet and deal with life after release.

The secret to building a successful relationship during and after incarceration is and always will be *true friendship*. Absolutely nothing else is both possible AND appropriate under these circumstances. In fact, such a relationship can be fine, beautiful, and rewarding. But the nitty-gritty of creating an intimate relationship—especially a healthy, lasting male/female relationship—cannot be accomplished until after release. If it is developed well and honestly then, it can become lasting and good.

Too often, however, prison romances remain melodramatic, clinging, dependent, and based on fantasy. This is deadly for the development of a lasting, intimate relationship—one that can deal with the issues of everyday life. A relationship built on illusion does not offer a useful foundation for life together "in the cold light of day." As a result, very few relationships survive the shift from prison to free society.

Therefore, a romantic relationship should be approached with great caution by both the inmate and the person outside of prison. In most cases, such a relationship is best avoided. Predictably, people involved in such interactions will not want to hear this. In fact, they may react with great resentment, telling you that their situation is "special" and lasting. In an effort to prove this, many insist on being married during imprisonment or immediately following release, only to discover they are now legally bound to a total stranger.

If you observe your loved one becoming involved this way, there may be little you can do. However, encourage them to keep a realistic perspective and refer them to reading materials and people who understand this aspect of the incarceration experience.

A WORD ON HELPING CHILDREN

Thus far, I have spoken mainly to adults who are members of a prisoner's closest circle of loved ones. Many in this circle, however, are children. These may be sons and daughters, sisters and brothers, nieces and nephews, or grandchildren.

As with an adult, the experience of having a loved one in prison affects a child's life in very important ways. Although the adult who cares for the child may realize this, it is hard to know what the effects will be or how to handle them. The caretaker is often uncertain because he or she doesn't know what the child feels about the situation and isn't sure what the child can understand or do to cope. Besides, the adult is also having difficulty dealing with the situation.

Although nothing has a 100% guarantee of success, the following information and guidelines can help a child cope positively with this experience. First of all, remember that children are simply people; they will be affected in much the same ways as adults.

Childhood Development

"As a tree is bent, so does it grow."

Children, even very young children, have the ability to give and receive information and to process that information in order to make sense of the world around them. Some of this information comes from the words and voice tones of the people close to them. Some information comes from what they personally see, hear, smell, taste, and feel. Children, in turn, react and interact with all of this information, which then becomes part of their total experience of life. They use this information to decide how they fit into the world and how they should react to events and the people around them.

From its experiences with others and from its thoughts while alone, a child develops answers to some of life's most important questions, such as: "How do I compare with others?" "What can I expect from others?" "What do others seem to expect from me?" "What do I have to do to keep the tension on me as low as possible in the situation in which I have to live?"

Of course, the way an infant or very young child processes this information is rather limited and crude compared to the methods a mature, healthy adult might use. Nevertheless, this early processing may strongly influence the final answers a child gives to these questions.

These answers may be based on truth and the way life is generally experienced by most people. If so, a child will tend to have positive experiences and will view life as worthwhile and fun. However, if the answers are untrue or unrealistic for most situations, the child will experience life as confusing, difficult, painful, or depressing.

Different Views of Life

Based on its interpretation of early experiences with the people close to it, a child may decide that people are not to be trusted because they bring pain, discomfort, and frustration to its life. If the child views most people this way in most situations, he or she may become unsociable, withdrawn, uncooperative, hard to know and get along with, and generally hostile toward society.

On the other hand, a child may decide from its early experiences that people are usually friendly and helpful and can be trusted to bring pleasure and relieve pain. This child is likely to make friends and be sociable, cooperative, and outgoing. He or she will want to get close to others and allow others to get close to him or her. This child will probably **not** be hostile toward society.

When a child decides not to trust people, we might think that the child has mis-interpreted his or her experiences. However, the child may have had experiences that justify such a negative interpretation. For example, if the people close to the child misunderstood its crying, they may have tried to feed it when it was in pain from having colic. In this case, it would be true that the adults did not relieve its pain. Or, if the adults are not present when the child needs care, the child may assume that it will always be abandoned by the people close to it.

In these examples, the child's decision was correct at the time. A child can feel the results of the situation, but may not be able to understand the causes. He or she can not understand that the adults made a mistake or perhaps could not be present due to sickness, work, or incarceration. Also, a child does not have a wide range of experiences to show that such negative events do not happen all the time. Thus, the child's negative interpretation may become "fixed."

Although the child may have felt hurt or frustrated sometimes or often, it is not true that everyone will hurt or reject him or her all the time. But if the child has "fixed" negative answers, he or she will respond negatively to most situations, even if the negative response is not appropriate. These inappropriate responses will continue even after the child is grown. Since he or she gives a negative response for no apparent reason, the child will probably feel he or she is "unacceptable" to others. In any situation, no matter how other people respond at first, this person will almost always do something which practically "forces" others to reject him or her.

Thus, a child who develops fixed negative responses to the world will find life unpleasant and unrewarding. It is possible for a person to change his or her answers to life's questions, but this is hard once these answers are fixed. A child has a much better chance for an enjoyable and satisfying life if the adults caring for him or her can help the child develop a realistic and positive view of life.

Dealing with Incarceration

"If you can make a positive adjustment to the absence of someone dear, it is more likely that the children in your care will also adjust successfully."

Just like an adult, a child will be affected by loss when a loved one is incarcerated. This loss can have a major impact on his or her process of making decisions about life. But the child will also be affected by how the significant adults in its life respond to this loss. The adult's ability to make sense out of what is happening has a strong impact on how a child might deal with its own experience. In fact, the adult can give the child a model from which it can learn how to help itself.

For example, as you the adult work through your own depression, anger, frustration, etc., you are showing the child that it is possible to deal with the grief of this experience. If you keep the lines of communication with the child open while you work through your feelings, the child has the chance to see that these feelings can be managed. This will help the child learn some effective ways to deal with painful feelings and cope with life's problems.

By observing your success in overcoming grief and making sense of a confusing and troubling situation, the child can develop a sense of hope. Then, when life feels like the "pits"—hard, painful, and confusing—he or she can still believe that the unpleasant experiences will eventually pass and be replaced by pleasant experiences once again. With this balanced perspective, the child is more likely to answer the basic questions about life and his or her place in the world in a positive way.

Guidelines

Guidelines to help a child deal with this experience are simple to state, but may not be easy to carry out.

- **First**, do not shield the child from the truth about the situation. The child can't make good decisions based on false, inaccurate, or partly true information. You do not need to be brutally frank with the truth. It is usually best to present it slowly, gently, and with compassion.

  It helps if the family and friends who are regularly involved with the child—as well as the incarcerated person—approve of telling him or her the truth. However, if you can't get their approval, you need to let them know that you are going to be truthful anyway. In this case, be ready for them to oppose you. But remember, it generally will harm the child in the long run if he or she is shielded now and has to learn the truth later.

- **Second**, when telling the child the truth, use words, expressions, and actions that the child can understand. This may take a lot of trial and error, but it can be done. Watch the child in other activities, especially in interactions with others. This will tell you what a particular child can understand. Then you can decide on the best approach to help that child make sense of this difficult situation.

- **Third**, observe the child the same way you observe yourself. Note any major changes in the child's way of doing things, in its moods, attitudes, etc. This is one of the best ways to detect when someone is having trouble going through the grief cycle. When you see the child is having trouble, try the same things that have helped you to move through your grief.

  If your methods don't seem to work for the child, get some advice. Talk to others who have gone through similar experiences with a child, or talk with your parents, grandparents, or friends. If none of this seems to help, go to a professional counselor, physician, or minister.

- **Fourth**, try to prepare the child for other people's reactions. Friends and acquaintances will certainly find out that the loved one is in prison, and some of them may react negatively. Help the child learn to describe the situation in a way that is honest but still comfortable for the child. At the same time, explain that he or she does not have to volunteer this information to everyone. You can help the child decide when and to whom the situation should be explained, and when it is not necessary or appropriate to offer this information.

You will need to give the child special support in dealing with other children. He or she must realize that children can be very cruel, particularly when they are in a group. You can help the child find a way to respond to cruel teasing without creating more resentment. In spite of their group behavior, some of these children may become good friends when dealt with alone. It is very important to remind the child that he or she is valuable as an individual: having a loved one in prison does not make the child a bad person.

- **Fifth**, help the child keep a balanced perspective if the prisoner displays any negative or unpleasant behavior in letters or during visits. Help the child realize the loved one is living in an "unreal" and troubling world. Do not, however, excuse bad or inappropriate behavior by the loved one. Instead, try to help the child differentiate between behavior and the person; explain that he or she can love the person without liking the behavior. And remember, children tend to copy the behavior they see in parents and other adults who are important to them. Therefore, negative behavior from the prisoner may encourage negative behavior in the child.

- **Sixth**, do not be startled if a child tries to "manipulate" the situation you are in for its own or the incarcerated one's benefit. Should this occur, talk straight to the child and try to reason things out. If this does not stop the pattern, get help from others, including, if necessary, a professionally trained therapist or physician.

- **Seventh**, give the child hope. Assure him or her that life will go on and that, no matter what has happened or will happen, life can still be good.

- **Eighth**, prepare the child for the loved one's return from prison. If the reunion triggers a return of the grieving process, help the child understand what is happening. The child needs to realize that the adjustment may be difficult, not only for the loved one who returns, but for those who have been waiting as well.

In some cases, the prisoner's release may mean that custody of the child will shift from you as caretaker to the returning loved one. This can be a very difficult transition for all of you and should be carefully prepared for in advance. In addition to practical details such as finances, housing, and schools, the change will require a great deal of emotional adjustment for the child, as well as for you and the returning loved one. Often it is better for the releasee to get at least somewhat settled in society and able to deal with his or her own personal adjustments before taking on the added responsibility of caring for a child.

Sometimes a caretaker is unwilling to give up custody because of a strong attachment to the child or because the parent seems unable to care for the child. This decision is a legal as well as a personal issue. It has very serious, long-term results since it affects the relationship between parent and child. It can have a powerful impact on how the parent and child view themselves and their place in the world. If maintaining custody has occurred to you, you should give it extremely careful thought. Then seek the objective advice of competent therapists and legal professionals before taking any further action.

Help Is Available

A note of caution. As is true for an adult, a child may seem to work through its grief very well and then have a relapse. This is not unusual. Stay calm and retain hope. Keep doing the things that you know have worked for you and the child in the past. Remember, what worked once will probably work again.

Whatever you do to deal with a child in this trying situation, remember to consider the level of his or her capabilities. Do not overestimate what he or she can do, but do not underestimate it either. Young children can and do solve rather complex problems. It has been my experience that most adults underestimate a child's ability rather than overestimate it.

However, it can have a bad effect on a child's development to go to the extreme in either overestimating or underestimating the child's capacity. If you are not sure of yourself in this matter, get advice from people who have more experience with children. It can be very helpful to get assistance from people who are professionally trained in grief resolution and personality development. It is also smart to talk with the child's teacher and school counselor to alert them to the unique needs resulting from this situation.

DEALING WITH THE SYSTEM

"The more you know about how the criminal justice system works, the more you will be able to get from it, and the more help you can give your loved one."

Strive to Learn

Learn all you can about how each part of the system works, how to get things done, who to call, etc. Never give up! You are the most important person in the world to your loved one. Believe this, even if your loved one has a negative reaction to your communications or visits.

Dealing with bureaucracy can be highly frustrating, whether it is with a jail, prison, parole board, or any other part of the criminal justice or welfare system. Remember that people who work in these jobs deal with many thousands of clients; they are often under pressure to do their job without enough staff or money.

To get information or action from any bureaucracy, you will need *persistence and perseverance.* Use any resource you can honestly reach. Don't get run off or turned off by the first person you contact, nor the second,the third, etc. Be creative when you can. Use humor when you can. Above all, be persistent, polite, and patient. Stick with it.

Pursue Your Rights

You have a right to accurate information and reasonable services, but be careful. If the person you contact gives you a hard time, acts rude, or fails to do what is required, don't argue with them. You may feel a lot of anger and frustration toward the bureaucracy or the staff members you contact, but do **not** vent it on them. This will rarely help you or your loved one get what you need. Hostility usually only breeds more hostility.

On the other hand, you should not have to accept abuse or tolerate bad manners or rudeness. Stand up for yourself and your rights. When dealing with a bureaucracy like the criminal justice system, it can be hard to find a balance between avoiding trouble and standing up for yourself. But the effort to find balance can help you build your confidence and check on your progress in working through your grief.

Again, the key ingredients for successful dealing with the system are patience and perseverance. Keep trying and you will often find someone else in the same office or system who can help you. Ask who can tell you what you need to know or who does have the authority to grant your reasonable request. Then go up the ladder of their organization until you find someone who will give you the service or information you are entitled to.

Always keep a record of who you communicate with, what they say, and when. Get the name and mailing address of key personnel. If necessary, write them a brief, courteous letter explaining your need or problem and asking how they can help. Keep a copy of your letter and send the original by certified mail, requesting a signed receipt to be sure they get it. If you don't get an answer in two weeks, follow up with another letter or a direct phone call. If your efforts are blocked by a subordinate, make it clear that you are requesting direct contact with the person in charge. Ask *how and when* you can get in touch with that person; if the subordinate is still not helpful, ask to be put in touch with his or her immediate supervisor.

Correctional officials should respond professionally to any **reasonable** questions or requests you make. If you do not get a reply after three attempts or the answer isn't reasonable, write to that person's superior asking for help; be sure to enclose copies of the letters you've already mailed and received. Above all, stick with it!

If you are relying on someone for help, do not build up your hopes unrealistically. What Yogi Berra said about a baseball game is also true about bureau-cratic decision-making: "It ain't over until it's over." Don't count your chickens before they hatch. Keep your perspective and your balance. The people advis-ing you may be competent and well-meaning, but still their forecasts may fail to work out as planned. Be sure to thank people for helping you even a little and, especially, for being civil and polite. A little sugar can go a long way in main-taining a useful relationship.

Top Priority

Remember, your *top priority* is to **genuinely take care of yourself**. If you work hard at this, you will be able to handle even the most frustrating experi-ences with the bureaucracy. You may not be able to force the prison or parole board to do what you want or what you think they ought to do, but you will feel better about yourself and what you are doing. Your relationship with your loved one will also tend to improve if you take care of your own health and happiness.

Taking genuine care of yourself will keep the grief process on track and *you* in control of your life. The time this takes will be different for each person, some-times a lot. You may begin to feel normal and be comfortable with your life and its routine. When you get bad visits, complaining letters, set backs from the parole board or courts, you can take them in stride. You are on top of your world.

You may think all the pain and trauma you have experienced is gone forev-er. But be cautious; this may not be true. Remember, your loved one is likely among the vast majority of prison inmates who will be released. While release is almost always eagerly awaited, it can also trigger a return of grief experiences.

THE HOMECOMING

"At first they may seem like a stranger, not someone you think you know really well! In truth, they have changed, and so have you."

Coming home is always a major adjustment for those who have been incar-cerated. It also requires major changes for those waiting at home. After all the hardship you've been through, you may believe your loved one's return will "fix" whatever problems exist in your life. But don't be surprised if this return actu-ally creates more problems than it fixes.

Reunions

Before his or her imprisonment, you may have been very dependent on the presence and support of your loved one. However, you have been doing with-out the presence of this person for many months or even years. You have worked hard to create your own way of doing things. You may not be prepared to change your new routines, even for a person you want in your life. And your returning loved one will not be in tune with your current habits and priorities. He or she may feel threatened and overwhelmed by so much sudden change. As a result, they may try to push people around, to insist on having things their way. He or she may expect, and even demand, that things go back to the way they were before incarceration.

If you have read **The Correctional Experience** section of this book, you will have some insight into the reasons for this kind of "power play." Although you understand, you must not accept any form of domination or abuse. This type of behavior will make it impossible to establish a healthy intimate relationship. If such behavior persists, insist that your loved one seek professional help to get his or her balance. Do NOT tolerate this type of behavior! Establishing a mutually satisfying relationship will require that all participants show a great deal of patience, understanding, and willingness to compromise.

Other members of the household or family may also have significant problems adjusting to the loved one's return. Children often need a lot of time, patience, and support to adapt to the arrival of someone home from prison. Caretakers, and the returning loved one, should do all they can to prepare children for the sudden reappearance of the former prisoner. The reunion should be as smooth, slow, and comfortable as possible, with the children assured that they are safe and loved.

Problems in adjusting to a loved one's sudden reappearance can vary widely among families. You may experience anything from mild annoyance to complete chaos. You may feel your life was finally running rather smoothly when your loved one showed up, but now things are rough, to say the least. When this happens, you may experience the return of feelings you had when your loved one was first incarcerated. Any change in life style or daily routine can be experienced as a significant loss.

Grief Can Start All Over

A return of the grief experience will certainly be frustrating and upsetting, but remember, you worked through it before. If you did it once, you can do it again. If and when you find your grief returning, keep calm, keep your perspective. Make plans to do the kind of things you did before to take care of yourself. If you have trouble working through the grief experience or run into obstacles putting your plans into action, you may need to get help. A good source of help would be someone professionally trained in grief and family systems counseling. Again, the first order of business is to take genuine care of yourself. Getting competent outside help may be necessary to accomplish this very important task.

In most cases, if you have resolved the grief problem once, you will not be side tracked if it returns. But it may catch you by surprise after your loved one's release because you aren't expecting it. Now that you have what you and your loved one wanted most—his or her return from prison—you know you "should" be happy, not upset. But keep in mind that adding another person to your household, especially after a long absence, is a major change in your life. And any major change in the context of living will always create problems that require adjustments. These adjustments, in part, may be experienced as loss, which then may bring a return of the grief experience. This experience could affect anyone who lives in the household.

Remember, this is natural. It is not abnormal for problems to arise when people reunite after an absence. So don't panic! Don't lose your perspective about what is true and real! Do go back to doing the kinds of things that helped you work through your grief before. Be calm and patient with yourself and with others who are involved in the adjustment. Build your "new relationship" on **true friendship**. And if your best efforts fail, do not hesitate to get outside professional help.

A FINAL WORD

In your struggles through the criminal justice maze, you should follow the last part of the Great Commandment, "Love your neighbor as yourself." In fact, this commandment simply describes the truth. You need to have love and respect for yourself in order to have love and respect for another. That is why it is so important that you take genuine care of yourself. This care shows that you love and respect yourself. I am not talking about being self-indulgent. Being self-indulgent is not healthy for either the long- or the short-term; in the long run, it is harmful. But you *must* do what it takes to stay healthy—physically, mentally, emotionally, and spiritually.

If you do take genuine care of yourself, you will be in the best possible position to follow the other universally good rule of life, the Golden Rule: "Do unto others as you would have them do unto you." Putting these principles in practice is the best and only way to be of genuine help to your loved one and yourself.

Please remember that no one was born knowing how to deal with the madness of the criminal justice maze. Your survival and growth demand a wealth of soul searching, honesty, and hard work. Keep your hope alive no matter how overwhelmed or depressed you may be. You can endure, and even profit, from the insanity and hardship of this experience. **Be of strong heart!**

ADDITIONAL READING

You may find the following books and sources of information helpful in working toward your personal growth. There are **many** other useful books and information sources, so look for them in bookstores, libraries, or by mail order. Also check the inside back cover of this book for a list of materials produced by OPEN, INC.

Anger

Murray Cullen, *Cage Your Rage: An Inmate's Guide to Anger Control.* 1992 ACA, 8025 Laurel Lakes Ct., Laurel MD 20707.

Jean P. Deschner. *The Hitting Habit: Anger Control for Battering Couples.* 1986. The Free Press, 866 Third Ave., New York NY 10022.

Education Resources

National University Continuing Education Association, One Dupont Circle, Washington DC 20036. *The Independent Study Catalog: NUCEA's Guide to Independent Study Through Correspondence Instruction.* 1989. Published for NUCEA by Peterson's Guides.

Peterson's Guide to Two-Year Colleges. 1992. And *Peterson's Guide to Four-Year Colleges.* 1992. Peterson's Guides, P.O. Box 2123, Princeton NJ 08543-2123.

You may also contact agencies such as the following for information about specific schools:

Association of Independent Colleges and Schools
One Dupont Circle, N.W., Ste. 350
Washington DC 20036

National Association of Trade and Technical Schools
750 First St., Ste. 900
Washington DC 20002

The Commission on Occupational Institutions—
Southern Association of Colleges and Schools
1866 Southern Lane
Decatur GA 30033

Your state education agency

Health

AIDS information: National AIDS Hotline 1-800-2437, or write National AIDS Clearinghouse, P.O. Box 6003, Rockville MD 20849-6003.

AIDS information as it relates to criminal justice: NCJRS (National Criminal Justice Referral Service), P.O. Box 6000, Rockville MD 20850, 1-800-851-3420.

Kenneth H. Cooper. *Aerobics.* 1990. Bantam, 666 Fifth Ave., New York NY 10103.

Paul Hauck. *Overcoming Depression.* New in paperback. Westminster Press, 100 Witherspoon St., Louisville KY 40202.

The T-Factor Gram Counter. Edited by Jamie Pope-Cordle and Martin Katahn. 1989. W.W. Norton Co., 500 Fifth Ave., New York NY 10110.

Meditation

Herbert Benson & Miriam Z. Klipper. *The Relaxation Response.* 1979. Avon Books, 1350 Avenue of the Americas, New York NY 10019.

Joseph Goldstein. *The Experience of Insight: A Simple & Direct Guide to Buddhist Meditation.* Shambhala, Horticultural Hall, 300 Massachusetts Ave., Boston MA 02115.

Lawrence LeShan. *How to Meditate: A Guide to Self-Discovery.* 1984. Bantam, 666 Fifth Ave., New York NY 10103.

Nilgiri Press, Box 256, Tomales CA 94971. Many excellent books available; write for catalog and ask about discount to prisoners.

Parenting for Inmates and Caretakers

Family Times. Wisconsin Clearinghouse, P.O. Box 1468, Madison WI 53701-1468. $8.95. Activities to strengthen family ties.

Keeping in Touch by Long Distance. Compiled by Ann Kerniski. Cornell Cooperative Extension, 1050 W. Genesee St., Syracuse NY 13204. $2.50. Packet of cards that suggest activities for keeping in touch.

Jan Walker. *Parenting from a Distance: Your Rights and Responsibilities.* 1987. The Interstate, P.O. Box 50, Danville IL 61834-4774. This book contains a reading list for separated families. Other corrections-related materials are also available from Interstate.

Books for young children with a parent in prison:

Martha W. Hickman. *When Andy's Father Went to Prison.* 1990. A. Whitman, 6340 Oakton St., Morton Grove IL 60053.

Donna Jones. *Joey's Visit.* 1988. Cornell Cooperative Extension, 1050 W. Genesee St., Syracuse NY 13204. $2.00.

Inez Maury. *My Mother and I Are Growing Strong.* (In English and Spanish.) New Seed Press, 1665 Euclid Ave., Berkeley CA 94709.

Recovery

Alcoholics Anonymous ("The Big Book"). AA World Services, 475 Riverside Dr., New York NY 10115. Also request a list of their other publications.

Patrick Carnes. *A Gentle Path Through the Twelve Steps.* 1989. CompCare Pubns., 2415 Annapolis Ln., Minneapolis MN 55441.

Hazelden Foundation, P.O. Box 176, Center City MN 55012-0176 (1-800-328-9000). Write (families can call) to request a free copy of their catalog of addiction-related materials.

Pia Mellody. *Facing Codependence.* 1989. Harper, Icehouse 1-401, 151 Union St., San Francisco CA 94111.

Edward J. Rydman. *Finding the Right Counselor for You.* 1989. Taylor Pub. Co., 1550 W. Mockingbird, Dallas TX 75235.

Relationships

Dale Carnegie & Dorothy Carnegie. *How to Win Friends and Influence People.* Pocket Books-Simon & Schuster, 1230 Ave. of the Americas, New York NY 10020.

Edwin H. Friedman. *Generation to Generation.* 1986. Guilford Press, 72 Spring St., New York NY 10012.

Harriet Goldhor Lerner. *Dance of Anger.* 1989. Harper Collins, Keystone Industrial Park, Scranton, PA 18512. And *Dance of Intimacy.* 1990. Harper Collins.

Maggie Scarf. *Intimate Partners: Patterns in Love & Marriage.* Ballantine Books, 201 E. 50th St., New York NY 10022.